The Contemporary Minstrel

Louis Anthony deLise

The Contemporary Minstrel

Songwriting, Recording and Making Money with Your Music

Bocage Music Publishing
Cherry Hill, NJ

Bocage Music Publishing
Cherry Hill, NJ

This book is a publication of
Bocage Music Publishing
Cherry Hill, NJ 08002-3002 USA

Telephone Orders   856-616-2867
Orders by e-mail   info@BocageMusicPublishing.com

ISBN-10: 0-692-30459-2
ISBN-13: 978-0-692-30459-4

Printed in U.S.A.

PUBLISHER	Bocage Music Publishing
DESIGNER	Theresa deLise, Caffeinated Brew Arts
COVER ART	Joseph A. Smargisso
COPY EDITOR and RESEARCH ASSISTANT	Elizabeth deLise

To my sons, Jonathan and James, who have tolerated a lifetime of experiencing me as being sometimes just a bit preoccupied as I glazed over contemplating yet another elusive phrase of some in-progress composition. Or, was I just wistfully remembering the silliness we shared playing baseball?

Contents

List of Tables

List of Examples

About the Author

Louis Anthony deLise (1949-) was born in Philadelphia and from age five grew up in rural Bucks County, Pennsylvania. He studied jazz drumming as a youngster and taught himself to play the piano by making up tunes and reading through fake books at the family spinet. He was greatly and forever influenced and inspired by his older brother, Michael, who let him sit in with his working band of older guys.

His formal studies in composition and percussion (he pursued a double major) began at Temple University in Philadelphia where he earned a Doctor of Musical Arts in composition.

While in music school, deLise wrote for local Philadelphia television programs and achieved his first *Billboard Magazine* "Pick Hit."

Fresh out of music school, deLise arranged and produced chart records for the J's and John Gibbs, including the hit, "J'Ouvert," for John Gibbs and The Jam Band (TEC/CBS Records) and, for the same label, co-produced and arranged a hit album for William DeVaughn that included three chart records and a co-write.

deLise founded the production music company, *MusiCrafters, Inc.*, for which he composed and produced hundreds of pieces, including award-winning productions for PBS, ABC, CBS and major corporations, like McNeil Pharmaceutical, Bristol-Meyers/Squibb, Sunoco and Pep Boys.

He worked for many years as a percussionist and arranger in the symphony pops orchestra of pianist Peter Nero. deLise gigged as a sideman in orchestras that accompanied Lou Rawls, Diana Ross, Luciano Pavarotti, Tom Jones and Tony Bennett.

deLise was arranger and conductor for Robert Hazard (writer of "Girls Just Wanna Have Fun") and Grammy® winners Patti LaBelle and Halestorm in concert performances and recordings. He arranged and conducted on two albums for Miss LaBelle: *Timeless Journey* and her number one hit, *The Gospel According to Patti LaBelle*. Additional songwriting and composing credits include albums and singles on the EMI, Vanguard, Def-Jam, Centaur and CBS record labels. His arranging and conducting work appears on albums alongside that of many of the country's top pop artists including, Carlos Santana, Sheila E., Wynonna Judd, Kanye West, CeCe Winans and Paul Shaffer.

A composer of concert music for choirs and instrumentalists, deLise's music is performed often and is available in print from Bocage Music Publishing and Print Music Source.

Louis deLise's most recent recordings include an album with his band, Philly Nouveau, an EP for his daughter, Liz de Lise and an album of his solo flute compositions recorded by flutist, John McMurtery.

Preface

This book was written in response to many requests from students and aspiring songwriters for a unified and organized approach to learning about songwriting.

My goal is to fill a perceived void in available educational materials. The text is based on my years of work as a composer, arranger, producer and songwriter and my experience as a teacher of music theory, arranging and songwriting at several colleges. These experiences are supplemented with research I have undertaken and still pursue in the areas of music, recording, lyric writing and creativity.

My methods for learning to compose songs are simple and traditional: carefully analyze what fine writers have created, listen to their works and emulate their efforts through lots of writing practice. Much trial and error has also gone into my learning. This, I presume, will be the experience of most ardent songwriting aspirants.

This is not a music theory text. Several fine books are available that present well the compositional techniques employed by composers of concert music. A bibliography in this book lists a few. My approach throughout the book, though, is to present aspects of music theory (and recording, production and business) as they naturally evolve in my discourse about the various songs and song forms I present.

Music theory is important. I encourage students to study thoroughly the subject and to develop general musicianship skills through ear training. Budding songwriters who are not as smitten with the study of theory as I can skip over those sections they do not find helpful for their personal musical style.

This is also not a book on orchestration or recording studio techniques. There are scholarly works available in these disciplines, too. However, in the course of attempting to explain fully the subject at hand, the craft of songwriting, I have found it necessary to examine and explain elements of these subjects as they relate to writing songs in today's music business.

Studying with a master musician remains an important part of any aspiring musician's experience, and one I highly recommend. Aspiring songwriters are today very fortunate to have at their disposal very low-cost access to original high-quality recordings of just about any composition one can imagine. I sincerely encourage anyone who wants to learn to write, in addition to analyzing, emulating, reengineering and studying with a good musician, to take the time and energy to listen actively to each of the examples included in this text.

Acknowledgements

This book would never have materialized had it not been for the indispensable assistance of two remarkable and wonderful women, both of whom I have the honor of loving: my daughter, Elizabeth, and my wife, Theresa. Thank you for the care, respect and integrity you each have brought as you helped research, edit, and design this text.

Theresa, thank you, especially, for the many, many hours you have devoted to helping me birth this and all my other "projects."

Special thanks to the persons who proofread drafts of this text: Maria Elena Contreras, Lora Lawrie and Michael Grassi.

Introduction

In Chapter One, I examine the interrelationship between melody and harmony and provide for the aspiring songwriter what I feel are the essential elements of Western music. I have chosen carefully the aspects of music theory that I present and have endeavored to explain those subjects in a clear, concise and understandable manner. I present the music theory essentials I believe one must know to compose songs in today's popular styles.

I recognize that theory study is an acquired taste and that many readers of this text will be comfortable with their level of attainment in musical skills. I invite those folks to consider at least doing a quick read of my take on the subject and then moving on to Chapter Two.

In Chapter Two, I begin to demonstrate how songwriters put music fundamentals to work to create relatively simple, but eternally great songs. Along the way, I introduce additional music theory material, including a few new scales and chords. I introduce the concept of form in music and examine three related song types that share an essential characteristic: each is composed of a single period. I include in this chapter a lengthy discussion of the Blues Form.

In Chapters Three, Chapter Four and Chapter Five, I demonstrate how periods can be joined together to produce longer song forms and examine the three Double Period song forms commonly used in pop music. In Chapter Three, I demonstrate and analyze the most commonly used song forms of the pop literature, the Verse/Chorus song and its variations.

I devote Chapter Four to a thorough examination of what I call the Twentieth Century Bar Form. Known also as bar form, rounded binary, or AABA, this was the most popular form for writers of America's Great American Songbook, the name given recently by commentators and performers for the loosely defined collection of songs created for Broadway musicals and Hollywood musical films produced during the 1930s, '40s and '50s. These are the songs that are referred to as standards and are often (some might say, too often), recorded.

In Chapter Five, I conclude my look at Binary Form songs with a discussion of songs in what I call Pop Song Binary Form. Pop Songs in this form are the second most common type to be considered a standard.

I devote Chapter Six to a discussion of the songwriting business. I look at why people write songs and what they do with them once they have been created. I present an overview of the music publishing, film and record business and how they relate to each other and the songwriter. I also discuss the present-day music business and how songwriters can navigate it to make an income from their songwriting.

My method for demonstrating how to compose good pop tunes is to analyze folk songs, songs from the pop literature, and a few songs of my composing. I believe one can learn what to do and what to avoid doing through thoughtful dissection of well-crafted songs.

I discuss lyric writing as an organic, integrated and integral part of the songwriting process. For each song form I present, I include an in-depth analysis of the lyrics. In addition, I devote all of Chapter Seven to an overview of many of the techniques I have observed in the lyric writing of several famous lyricists.

Some may question my choices of songs for analysis, especially since I include very old songs or songs that are not well known. Here is the thing: Well-done is well-done. My analysis will revolve around musical form, the construction of the melody, the lyrics and the harmony. These aspects of composing change little from generation to generation. What changes are the ways these important features are presented in the musical arrangement, and if a song is recorded, in the production.

My hope for all serious aspiring songwriters who use this text is that they evolve a personal method for analyzing and reengineering songs; that they begin to listen with new ears and *truly hear* what other songwriters have crafted into existence. Further, by understanding even a little bit about the arcane details of the business of music, I am hopeful that uninitiated songwriters will be able to protect themselves from the myriad obstacles and pitfalls of this wonderfully amazing, but typically unforgiving music industry.

Louis Anthony deLise
Cherry Hill, New Jersey
30 August 2014

CHAPTER ONE

MELODY

 It's quite amazing! Even though music surrounds us at every turn, even though we "know what we like when we hear it," it is almost impossible, even for musicians, to explain succinctly what it is that makes a particular tune resonate. We hear, remember and sing along with the songs, symphonies and jingles that wash over us each day, but what is it that allows these melodies to stick?

Some tunes endure for centuries. "Shenandoah," "Silent Night," "New Britain" (The hymn tune sung to the text, "Amazing Grace"), "Ode to Joy," "O Sole Mio," "On Top of Old Smoky," "Beautiful Dreamer," "Londonderry Air," and "Happy Birthday" are melodies that remain popular even though all were created many years ago. And remember, each of these tunes was introduced at a time when there was no mass audio communication.

Of course, it is the *melody* that has kept these songs popular for generations. It is not the song's production that we whistle as we work; it is the melody that we parrot. Sure, the *rhythm* of the melody is uniquely important, as are the lyrics. It is the particular succession of pitches presented in a particular rhythm (perhaps sung to a particular lyric), what we call the melody, which becomes etched in our memory.

In this chapter, I will provide some insight into what makes melodies endure and how you can go about refining your melodic gifts. I will share with you my thoughts about why some melodies have become part of the fabric of our lives. I will do so through a thoughtful analysis of some exceptional music. This careful examination of the techniques other songwriters have employed will provide guidelines for your songwriting.

NOTE

For most of us, describing why one melody works and another one does not is like explaining why we like vanilla ice cream rather than strawberry, or why blue is our favorite color.

WHAT IS A MELODY?

A *melody* is a coherent horizontal series of single tones that floats above the *harmony* and is anchored by the rhythm and meter. In a pop song, the melody carries with it the short narrative of the song's lyric.

Melody is distinct from harmony in that the pitches used to create harmony occur as vertical simultaneities. It is distinct from *rhythm* in that the sounds making up a melody are pitched; the frequencies of a melody are clear, regular and stable enough to be heard as something other than noise.

Rhythm is the part of music concerned with duration of sounds and how those sounds are accented, or stressed, with some sounds performed at a louder volume than other sounds. It is impossible to separate rhythm and harmony from melody. The duration of each of the pitches in a melody's series of horizontal tones and the relative weight of each pitch is integral to how impressive a melody is, and therefore how it will be recognized as special and memorable. I will write more about the uses of harmony and rhythm in pop music in a subsequent chapter.

The idea of melody making evolved from speaking. It was likely influenced by the songs of birds and other animals. The anthropologist and ethnomusicologist, Steven Feld, found that the Kaluli people of the Southern Highlands Province of Papua New Guinea believe that human speech is for utilitarian purposes, whereas bird song (translated by humans into weeping, poetics and song) is for conveying feelings. It is easy to imagine melody then as a heightened form of speaking, especially when one considers that normal speech also occurs in rhythm with the speaker's voice rising and falling in pitch to provide interest, variety and emphasis.

INTUITION

Creating a potent melody is an intuitive act... a mysterious process.

For the gifted songwriter, creating a potent melody is an intuitive act; the creative act is a mysterious process where the composer, drawing on a thorough knowledge of chord patterns and melodic gestures, hears in her inner ear, and then commits to paper or recording, what the world will laud as beautiful. Indeed, knowledge fuels intuition. An expert songsmith will have a command of *harmonic motion* (chord progressions), *melodic gestures* (the implied meaning of a melody), *musical contour* (the shape of a melody—how it goes higher and lower), *form* (how phrases are managed), and *development* (the way composers manipulate important musical material). Obtaining this knowledge is necessarily a matter of study, analysis and listening.

STUDY, ANALYSIS AND LISTENING

I am always stunned to meet people who aspire to create their own songs, but know little or nothing about music. These folks think that their ambition alone will somehow provide them the wherewithal to create hit songs.

It's not that one needs to be a master performer or music theorist to write a hit; rather you need to be expert in something. For instance, in my professional experience of working as a musical arranger and record producer, I have worked with folks who possess very little formal musical knowledge, who haven't been expert performers or trained composers, but who were, perhaps, expert listeners. Through their listening, and singing along as they listen, they have discerned what it is that makes music work. They might not be able to articulate in musical terms why they do what they do, but they are able to intuit how to take the germ of a musical (and perhaps lyrical) idea and successfully shape it into a fully formed song. They hone their melodic gifts by listening and singing along to music that others have composed. Listening and singing along to famous songs is foundational for a songwriter's musical education.

Studying the material presented here will provide an additional level of professionalism, as will working with an experienced master musician. I have met many competent singers, instrumentalists and aspiring songwriters who were certain that they would have achieved greater success had they had the opportunity to study with a master musician.

NOTE

In my recording and performing career, I have never met anyone who alleged that his or her musical prowess was stymied by having formally studied music.

ANALYSIS: MUSICAL FORENSICS

To analyze any song, we will take it apart to see what makes it tick.

We will identify the smaller sections of the melody (its *motives* and *phrases*), examine how each pitch relates to the others in the melody and to the harmony and determine the rhythm of the melody (its *melodic rhythm*) and the shape of the melody (the *melodic contour*).

Later, we will look at how the sections of songs work together and how those sections are repeated, modified or dismissed. This is the *form* of the song. We will also examine the overall rhythm of the song, its *meter* and the *tempo* in which the song is usual heard. (I discuss meter and tempo at length in Chapter Two). The way the chords of a song progresses one to another and the rhythm of this progression of chords will also be a subject for our analysis. This is the song's *harmonic rhythm*.

This chapter will conclude with a set of exercises that will provide the reader an opportunity to create some short melodies by using the information I have presented about how melodies and harmonies work together.

THE COMPONENTS OF MELODY:
INTERVALS, SCALES, AND HARMONY

It is easy for most of us to recognize a melody when we hear one. In a song, it is the part to which the words are sung. We hear the pitches of a melody as a shape that takes us as listeners on a journey. A melody's curve helps create tension and then resolution. From the beginning, we ride a melody's crest from one emotion to another until expectation leads us as listeners to resolution at the melody's end.

In the following sections, I will introduce you to some of the components of melody and to harmony: individual tones that are sounded together or in close proximity. *Rhythm*, the way pitches flow through time, will be introduced and further discussed in subsequent chapters.

INTERVAL SIZE

The distance between two pitches is called an *interval*. Intervals are measured in terms of their *numerical size* (the number of *diatonic* scale steps or *musical alphabet* letter names the two pitches span), and the number of semitones or half steps (the smallest interval in the Western system) is between the two pitches.

The seven white keys of the piano keyboard (the natural keys) correspond to the seven letter names of the musical alphabet: A, B, C, D, E, F, and G. The five black keys of the keyboard are the chromatic keys.

Example 1: Musical Alphabet

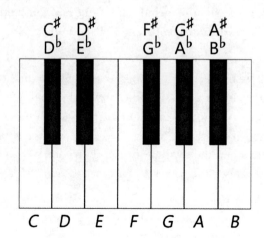

Intervals are expressed as a number with a qualifying adjective, like this: major second, minor third or perfect fifth. The number part of this expression is determined by counting the letter names that an interval spans. C to C is a *prime* or *unison*, C to D is a *second*, C to E is a *third*, C to F is a *fourth*, C to G is a *fifth*, C to A is a *sixth*, C to B is a *seventh* and C to the C eight steps higher is an *octave*.

The intervals of a fourth, fifth and octave above the C are called *perfect* intervals. The others, a second, third, sixth and seventh are called *major*. When perfect intervals are made smaller by a half step, they become *diminished*. A major interval reduced by a half step becomes *minor*; a minor interval reduced by a half step becomes diminished. Both perfect and major intervals if made larger by a half step become *augmented*.

Table 1: Modifying Intervals

-2 half-steps	-1 half-step	Starting Interval	+1 half-step	+2 half-steps
-	Diminished	**Perfect**	Augmented	-
Diminished	Minor	**Major**	Augmented	-
-	Diminished	**Minor**	Major	Augmented

In other cultures, musicians use smaller intervals like quartertones. Some pop singers, especially jazz and blues singers, purposely sing intervals that are smaller than half steps to affect *blue notes*. Other singers have been known to sing quartertones accidentally (but that is the subject for another discussion and beyond the scope of this text)!

Intervals that occur in succession are called *melodic intervals*. Those that occur simultaneously (vertically) are called *harmonic intervals*. It will no doubt appear obvious to you that melodic intervals are fundamental to melody writing just as harmonic intervals are fundamental to forming the harmonic underpinning of tunes.

Intervals up to a *perfect octave* (twelve half-steps) are considered *simple intervals*. Those intervals greater than an octave are considered *compound intervals*. It is common to call the compound interval of an octave plus a fourth an *eleventh*, and an octave plus a sixth a *thirteenth*.

The distinctive sound quality of each interval is significant. You will find learning to identify each sound quality by ear to be an important skill. Like all skills, being able to identify the intervals you hear, sing, and play can be developed through drill.

Intervals of all qualities can be found within the context of the various scale formulations. Perfect (Example 2), Major (Example 3) and Minor (Example 4) intervals can be found between the various pitches of the C major scale.

NOTE

Evolution of the G-clef:

Example 2: Perfect Intervals of the C Major Scale Plus Augmented 4th

NOTE

Intervals must be named in two respects: the number of steps between the two pitches and the quality – major, minor, diminished, or augmented.

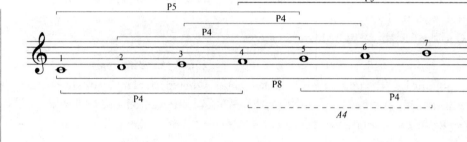

Example 3: Major Intervals of the C Major Scale

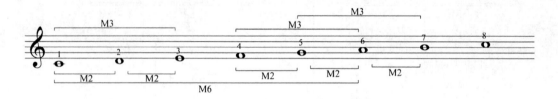

Example 4: Minor Intervals of the C Major Scale

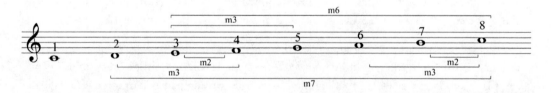

Within one octave of the major scale, one will find these intervals: perfect prime (unison), major second, minor second, major third, minor third, perfect fourth, perfect fifth, major sixth, minor sixth, minor seventh, major seventh, perfect octave and the augmented fourth.

Melody   7

Interval quality is abbreviated as follows:

Table 2: Interval Quality

Interval Quality	Abbreviation
Major	M
Minor	m
Perfect	P
Augmented	A
Diminished	d

Here is a chart of intervals measured in half steps:

Table 3: Interval Names

Half-Steps	Interval Names
0	Perfect Unison (Perfect Prime)
1	Minor Second (Half Step)
2	Major Second (Whole Step)
3	Minor Third
4	Major Third
5	Perfect Fourth
6	Augmented Fourth / Diminished Fifth
7	Perfect Fifth
8	Augmented Fifth / Minor Sixth
9	Major Sixth
10	Minor Seventh
11	Major Seventh
12	Perfect Octave

Intervals up to a *perfect octave* (eleven half steps) are considered *simple intervals*. Those intervals greater than an octave are considered *compound intervals*. It is common to call the compound interval of an octave plus a fourth an *eleventh*, and an octave plus a sixth a *thirteenth*.

Enharmonic Equivalence

Some intervals span the same number of half steps, but are named differently because they span different letter note names.

For instance, C up to G$^\sharp$ spans eight half steps, and since C to G spans five letter names, this interval is considered a fifth. In this example, it is called an *augmented fifth*.

Now consider the interval C up to A$^\flat$. This interval spans the same eight half steps as our previous example. Because C to A spans six letter names, this interval is considered a sixth. In this example, C up to A$^\flat$ is called a *minor sixth*.

Pitches that are named differently, but represent the same frequency, are said to be *enharmonically equivalent*. In our example, A$^\flat$ and G$^\sharp$ are different names for a pitch of the same frequency. The way we name each pitch is dependent on the context. In pop music, this means that notes are named based on an analysis of the scale in which the song (or part of the song) is written. The same pitch will be called A$^\flat$ when it functions as scale degree 2, the *supertonic*, of the G$^\flat$ major scale, but will be called G$^\sharp$ when it functions as scale degree 3, the *mediant*, of the E major scale. We will see in our continued analysis that function is an important consideration when determining the features of a section of music.

Treble Staff

The examples in this book are almost all written on a *treble staff*. The staff provides a convenient graphic representation of the sounds used in music. The treble staff uses a *treble clef*, also called a G-clef. It defines the second staff line as the pitch, "G." Using the musical alphabet, one can easily define the names of the rest of the staff's lines and spaces. The spaces are named F, A, C, and E; the lines of the staff are named E, G, B, D, and F. There are several other clefs used in music. The treble clef will serve our purposes for now.

SCALES AND KEYS

Melodic and harmonic material is organized into collections of pitches called *scales*. Scales are organized based on the intervallic relationships between the scale degrees. The most commonly used scales in Western music are the *major scale* and the *minor scale*. The minor scale is used in three varied forms: *natural minor*, *harmonic minor* and *melodic minor*. The formula for the intervallic relationships of a major scale is shown in Example 5.

Major scales can be replicated in either direction, ascending or descending, using the same whole step/half step formula.

Minor scales are not so straight forward, as there are three forms or formulae for minor scales: the natural minor (Example 6), the harmonic minor (Example 7) and the melodic minor (Example 8).

Example 5: C Major Scale

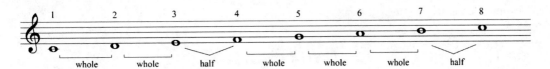

Example 6: C Natural Minor Scale

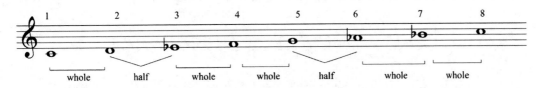

Example 7: C Harmonic Minor Scale

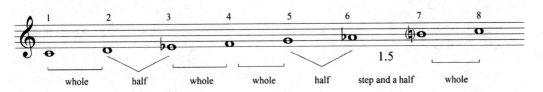

NOTE

The interval between any two adjacent black and white keys on the piano keyboard is a half step. There is also a half step between B to C and E to F.

Example 8: C Melodic Minor Scale

NOTE

Intervals are said to possess one of five sound qualities: major, minor, perfect, augmented, or diminished.

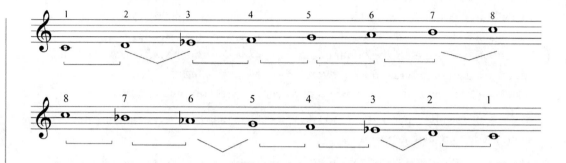

Scales are named by their first degree or pitch. The major scale demonstrated above begins on the pitch C. It is therefore called a *C major scale*. A piece of music, or a section of a piece of music, that primarily uses the pitch collection of a single scale, is said to be *in the key* of that scale. Thus, a song that primarily uses the pitch collection of the C major scale is said to be in the *key of C major*.

OTHER SCALES

There are many other scales used in Western popular songs. These include *pentatonic scales*, *chromatic scales*, and the *Dorian, Phrygian, Lydian, mixolydian* and *Aeolian* modes. Those collections and formulae will be discussed in a subsequent chapter.

CONSONANCE AND DISSONANCE

Intervals are further characterized as being either *consonant* or *dissonant*. Consonant intervals are major and minor thirds, perfect fifths, and major and minor sixths. All seconds, sevenths, fourths, and the augmented and diminished versions of fifths are considered dissonant. In his excellent music theory text, *The Complete Musician*, the theorist Steven G. Laitz provides an additional refinement. Laitz calls perfect octaves and perfect fifths, *perfect consonances*. Major and minor thirds and major and minor sixths are *imperfect consonances*.

Although consonance and dissonance are to some extent in the ear of the hearer and a function of acculturation, some music theorists believe that humans possess a genetic predisposition to sounds we consider consonant or dissonant. In his book, *This is Your Brain on Music*, Daniel J. Levitin notes that infants show a preference for consonance over dissonance. Levitin proffers that an appreciation for dissonance usually evolves later in life as one matures. This might be true; nevertheless, many listeners develop little tolerance for dissonant melodic and harmonic intervals. Instead, they experience dissonant melodies and dissonant chords as unpleasant. Like musical context, cultural context is a key factor in developing aural perception. A perceived unpleasantness of dissonance is probably why so few Alban Berg or Ornette Coleman tunes have broken into the *Billboard* "Hot 100."

The concept of what we perceive as consonant or dissonant musical sounds has evolved over the centuries. Further, we might hear the same sounds as consonant in one context and not in another. In this way, the perception of an interval's relative consonance or dissonance is a function of the musical context in which it is sounded.

Let's listen to the interval of the major seventh. The interval of a major seventh, for instance the interval of middle C to the B-natural above it, is heard as very dissonant. The inversion of the major seventh, the minor second (middle C to the B-natural a half step below it) is also heard as a biting dissonance in our Western culture. However, when sounded along with the pitches of a major triad to form what you will learn to be a *major seventh chord*, this interval sounds quite pleasant, enough so that it is used continually in popular music, including as the concluding chord of many songs.

Listen, for instance, to the song, "Garota de Ipanema" ("The Girl From Ipanema"), written by composer, Antônio Carlos Jobim (1927-1994), and lyricists, Vinícius de Moraes (1913-1980) and Norman Gimbel (1927-). This song is thought to be the second most recorded song in history, after John Lennon (1940-1980) and Paul McCartney's (1942-), "Yesterday."

The underlying harmony of the first measure of "The Girl from Ipanema" is a major seventh chord. Coincidentally, like the Beatles' song, "Yesterday," the melody of the Jobim song begins on the second degree of the scale, but unlike "Yesterday," the melody of "Ipanema" does not resolve downward to the first degree of the scale, as would be customary. Instead, it floats down to the seventh degree of the scale, also known as the *leading tone.*

Most startling to classically trained ears, instead of resolving upward to the first degree of the scale (as all good leading tones are supposed to do), Jobim moves the melody back to its starting point, scale degree 2, as shown in Example 9.

NOTE

A recording of the song, "The Girl from Ipanema," made by Stan Getz and Astrud and João Gilberto, was the Grammy® Award's Record of the Year in

Example 9: "The Girl from Ipanema"

The Girl from Ipanema

Music by
Antonio Carlos Jobim
Lyrics by
Vinicius de Moraes and Norman Gimbel

Harmony

Melodies of pop-style songs usually exist in a mutually dependent relationship with an underlying harmony. Harmony in this instance refers to the chords that accompany a melody. You hear harmony underpinning melodies in many recorded pop songs. The chords played on the guitar or piano, sounded in the string and horn section, or sung by the back-up vocalists generally supply the harmony in these recordings.

Building Chords

The term *chord* is the name given to three or more pitches arranged vertically and sounded more or less simultaneously. When all the chord tones are sounded at once, the chord is called a *block chord*. When the chord tones are sounded in rapid succession, but heard as part of the same musical unit, the chord is said to be *arpeggiated*.

Three-note chords are called *triads*. Chords with more than three pitches are called *added note chords*. Chords made up strictly of scale tones stacked a third apart are called *diatonic chords*. Example 10 shows all the diatonic triads found using the notes of the C major scale.

Example 10: Diatonic Triads

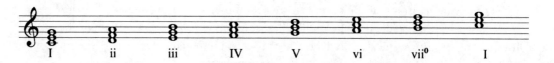

I   ii   iii   IV   V   vi   vii°   I

You will notice that all of the diatonic triads are composed of three pitches that are a third apart. For example, the I chord is composed of C, E, and G; the ii chord—D, F, and A, and so on. You will find that stacking thirds one upon another is an easy way to build up chords.

Naming the Parts of a Chord

The notes that make up a chord are often called *voices*. The lowest voice of a triad is called the *root*. The middle voice is called the *third* or *chord third*; the top voice of a triad is called the *chord fifth* or simply, the *fifth*. The two voices above the root are so named because they are a third and a fifth above the chord's root.

Naming Chords

Chords are named for their root and for their *quality*. In this context, quality refers to the sound quality of the chord. We've already discovered that chords can be built up by stacking thirds one on top of the other. The kinds of thirds used and the order in which they are used will determine the quality of a chord.

As you will see, musicians are fond of identifying the elements of music in multiple ways. Chords can also be named according to their function and the scale degree on which they are constructed. The degrees of the scale are numbered and named.

Here's a handy chart that provides the scale degree and its formal name:

Table 4: Diatonic Scale Degree Formal Names

Diatonic Scale Degree	Formal Name
1	Tonic
2	Supertonic
3	Mediant
4	Subdominant
5	Dominant
6	Submediant
7	Leading tone

A chord built on the first degree of the scale, where scale degree 1 is the root of the chord, can be called a *tonic triad*. A triad built on scale degree 2, a *supertonic triad*, and so on.

In our analysis of chords, we will use Roman numerals as a shorthand method to describe chords. Normal-size Roman numerals will be used to mean major chords; small Roman numerals (e.g., vi) will be used to mean minor chords. Diminished chords are indicated using small numerals and the degree sign (e.g., vii⁰). Augmented chords are symbolized in this method by using a numeral and a plus sign (e.g., V⁺).

Building a Major Triad

Placing a *major third* above the root and a *minor third* above that creates a major triad. Put another way, the interval between the chord root and the chord third is a major third. The interval between the chord third and the chord fifth is a minor third. A major triad built on C will contain the pitches C, E, and G.

BUILDING A MINOR TRIAD

A minor triad is constructed by placing a minor third above the root and a major third above that. Put another way, the interval between the root and the chord third is a minor third. The interval between the chord third and the chord fifth is a major third. A minor triad built on C will contain the pitches C, E$^\flat$ and G.

BUILDING A DIMINISHED TRIAD

A diminished triad is constructed by placing two minor thirds, one above the other. A diminished triad built on C will contain the pitches C, E$^\flat$ and G$^\flat$.

BUILDING AN AUGMENTED TRIAD

An augmented triad is constructed by placing two major thirds, one above the other. An augmented triad built on C will contain the pitches C, E and G$^\sharp$.

Example 11 shows triads of each quality, and all built on the root, C.

Example 11: Quality of Triads

Using the naming rule above, the chords in this example are named: C major, C minor, C diminished, and C augmented.

HIERARCHY OF DIATONIC CHORDS IN TONAL MUSIC: THE PRIMARY TRIADS

Tonal music ascribes special importance to three of the chords used to harmonize major scale or minor scale melodies. Called *primary triads* or *chords*, these are the chords built on the tonic, the subdominant and the dominant degrees of the scale.

The one chord (I), the four chord (IV), and the five chord (V) as they are named by pop musicians are often heard as the pillars of a composition. It is quite possible to create very successful songs using only these three chords as the harmonic basis.

The three primary chords form the essential underpinning of many successful songs and include songs in blues form, hymn tunes, and many pop and rock songs. I write "essential" because songwriters often modify the primary chords by adding other *color tones*, like sixths, sevenths and seconds. These added notes change the sound of the chords, but do not alter the chord's function. We'll look at their use in a subsequent section on chord progressions.

The primary chords provide the basis for a standard blues pattern, as shown in Example 12.

NOTE

The three primary chords form the essential underpinning of many successful sonas ...

Example 12: Basic Blues Chord Pattern

CHORD SYMBOL NOTATION

Chords are represented in sheet music using a shorthand method called *chord symbol notation*. Chord symbols indicate the root of the chord, the quality of the chord, any added color tones, and what chord member is to be played in the bass (the lowest pitch in a chord).

ADDED NOTES

Several different notes can be added to a chord. These are indicated as a number that represents the interval between the root of the chord and the added note. For instance, a sixth added to a C chord will be represented as C^6. A musician seeing this symbol will sound a C major triad, with the interval of a diatonic (major) sixth added above the bass. In other words, she will play the pitches C, E, G, and A, the added 6th above the bass. Most commonly, one will see a seventh added to a chord. This means to add the interval of a minor seventh above the root. In a C^7 chord the pitches C, E, G and B^b would be sounded. A capital letter alone tells one to play a major chord in root position with no added notes.

Note in Example 13 that there can be multiple symbols for a chord.

Example 13: Chord Symbols Commonly Found in Lead Sheets

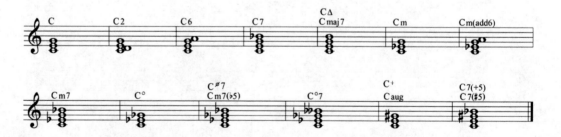

LEAD SHEETS

A lead sheet is a simplified document used to represent music on paper. The typical lead sheet will provide the song's melody written on a treble staff, the lyrics of the song, and the harmony notated in chord symbol notation. The *lead sheet* will also usually provide an idea of the tempo and style of the song (the rate of speed at which it is to be performed), and should indicate the composer, lyricist, and copyright ownership information. As in Example 14, all the musical examples in this book are written as lead sheets.

Example 14: "The Lead Sheet Song"

The songwriter and singer, Hank Williams (1923-1953), made thorough use of the three primary chords in his many hit songs. The first sixteen measures of his song, "Your Cheatin' Heart," (Example 15) use only the primary chords.

Example 15: "Your Cheatin' Heart"

Chord Progressions: Harmonic Motion

Chords move from one to another in goal oriented and predictable ways. The predictability of chord progressions is the result of tone tendency, goal orientation and conditioning. Tone tendency, simply put, is the likelihood that a pitch will tend to move in one direction or another, based on its position in the scale and expectations generated because of conditioning: we have heard scale degrees move in a particular way before and therefore expect that they will do so again.

In pop-style songs, chord progressions are governed by the tone tendency of the lowest voice of a chord, the *base*, forming what musicians call a *bassline*.

The ultimate goal of nearly all chord progressions is to come to rest at the end of a piece of music on the tonic harmony. In the meantime, between the beginning of the song and its end, chords move from one to another in well-established patterns and, often, predictable ways.

Note

Does this mean that the chord progressions of all songs are absolutely predictable? No, it does not. In fact, one goal of a good songwriter is to create new chord patterns that are typically the

IT'S ALL ABOUT THE BASS: BASIC CHORD MOVEMENT

In pop-style songs, chords progress from one to another based in patterns of root movements established by the songwriter. Chord root movement patterns are most often scalar (they follow a scale or part of a scale either up or down), based on root movements by fourths (e.g., roots moving from D to G to C), movement by third (e.g., thirds falling from C to A to F to D), or most usually some combination of these.

Scalar root movement is pretty obvious on its face: The chord roots simply ascend or descend following the pattern of a scale or part of a scale. The movement of chord roots by fourths mimics the very important progression of the dominant chord (V) to the tonic chord (I) that is found as the concluding progression of so many songs. The falling thirds or ascending thirds root movement follows chord arpeggiation or partial chord arpeggiation.

INVERSIONS

Movement in the bass is also created when notes other than the root are placed in the lowest voice. When a chord is presented with its third, fifth or seventh in the bass, it is said to be *inverted*. When the root is in the bass, the chord is in *root position*, when the third is in the bass, it is in *first inversion*, when the fifth is in the bass, it is in *second inversion*. When the seventh of a chord is in the bass, the chord is said to be in *third inversion*. Example 16 shows the first and second chord inversions.

Example 16: Chord Inversions

Often Heard Chord Progressions

Why study chord progressions? Songs need to begin somewhere. In my experience as a record producer and arranger working with other songwriters and bands, I have observed that songs tend to begin in one of a few ways. Sometimes a songwriter will begin with a chord progression or a part of one. Sometimes the starting point is a *melodic motive*: a short, rhythmically unique melodic phrase. I often begin a new song with a *lyrical hook* idea. I found this particularly useful when I worked as a jingle writer. A lyrical hook is a single short phrase that usually includes the title of the song. I have also worked with bands that build up songs that are based on a musical accompaniment riff, like an electric bassline or guitar lick. The terms *riff* and *lick* are used to mean motives that occur in the accompaniment. The remainder of this chapter is devoted to chord progressions. We'll examine motives and lyrics in a later chapter.

While some might think that writing songs with "standard" chord progressions is uninteresting, I believe the contrary can be true. Besides, all art is *intertextual*: it references other art.

In his seminal book on intertextuality, Michael Klein writes,

> "The frontiers of music are never clear-cut: beyond its framing silence, beyond its inner form, it is caught up in a web of references to other music: its unity is variable and relative. Musical texts speak among themselves."

In the hands of a master songsmith, "stock" progressions can be combined, varied and reworked in wonderfully creative ways to produce fresh sounding accompaniments for newly composed songs.

Note that many of the clichéd chord changes or chord progressions that I am about to present can be combined.

In the following examples, I provide both the chord symbol notation and the Roman numeral analysis. For now, we'll look at chord progressions in major keys. We will turn our attention to minor key chord progressions and songs a bit later.

Scalar Ascending: I—II—III—IV

The great Beatles song, "Here, There and Everywhere," written by John Lennon and Paul McCartney, features an ascending scalar chord progression that supports the beautiful melody during the first five measures Example 17.

Example 17: "Here, There and Everywhere"

In the example, the roots of the accompanying harmony progress through the first four degrees of the G major scale, forming a bassline that serves as a *counterpoint* to the melody. The term, counterpoint, refers to a secondary melodic line that is sounded at the same time as the primary melody.

The two lines are interdependent. Bass lines in pop tunes are often melodic, prominent and important enough to be heard as contrapuntal. The contrapuntal effect is more obvious in a song like "Piano Man."

SCALAR DESCENDING: I—V⁶—IV⁶—I⁶₄—IV—I⁶—II

"Piano Man," (Example 18) by the composer Billy Joel (1949-), employs a bassline that descends through an entire major scale. In Example 19, the bassline is not composed of the chord roots, but instead is made up of other chord tones. Joel uses chords in inversion to create a bassline that descends through the first seven notes of the major scale.

Placing a voice other than the root of a chord in the bass is a common practice in both concert and pop music. As described previously, this is called inversion. Inverted chords are indicated in sheet music with a slash. For example, G/B indicates to the musician that she should play a G triad with B in the bass.

Example 18: "Piano Man"

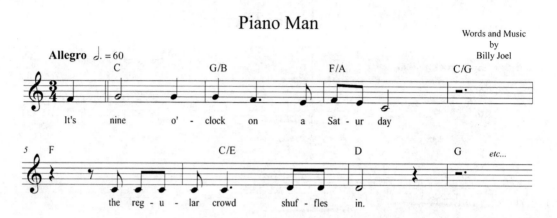

Example 19: Chord Progression for "Piano Man"

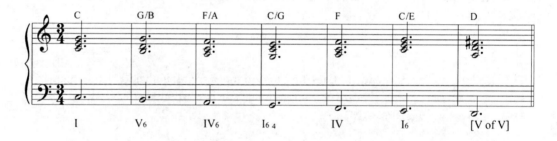

"Wake Me When September Ends" (Example 20) was written and released in 2005 by the band, Green Day. It was written as a collaborative effort of the band. The band's lead singer, Billie Joe Armstrong (1972-), created the lyrics.

Like Billy Joel's "Piano Man," "Wake Me When September Ends" was also written using a descending scalar bassline. The writers of this song chose to harmonize their descending bassline differently than did Billy Joel. During the first five measures of the song, Billie Joe Armstrong and his co-writers create a bassline that descends from the tonic, through the leading tone and submediant, to the dominant and then to the subdominant, all the while sounding a G power chord.

Notice the new chord symbols featured in this song: G⁵. These indicate *power chords*. Power chords do not contain a chord third. They are played on the fifth and sixth strings of an electric guitar. Power chords are *dyads*, two-note chords. The power chord/dyad in "Wake Me" is composed of G and D.

In measure six, the creators of "Wake Me" sound a *chromatic harmony*. A chromatic harmony is one that does not exist in the key of the song. In this case, the chromatic chord, C-minor, is borrowed from the parallel minor key, G-minor. The subdominant of G-minor is C-minor. Using borrowed chords is a common feature of pop music.

Example 20: "Wake Me When September Ends"

FALLING THIRDS: I—vi—IV—V

The root motion of the chord progression I—vi—IV—V outlines an arpeggiated subdominant triad that resolves to the dominant. In C major, the pitches found in the subdominant triad are F, A, and C. The root movement of the chord progression I—vi—IV (C—A—F) outlines the subdominant triad in reverse. Because the IV chord leads nicely to the dominant harmony, in this case, G, the progression I—vi—IV progresses very convincingly to V. The progression of subdominant (IV) to dominant (V) to tonic (I) is very strong and an essential progression in the tonal music of our Western musical culture. It has been presented before in the song, "Your Cheatin' Heart." You'll see this progression again…, again…, and again!

"Bristol Stomp" (Example 21) is one of many songs from the 1950's and 1960's that used the I—vi—IV—V chord progression as its foundation. Here is a song that made it to number two on *Billboard* "Hot 100." A 1961 recording of "Bristol Stomp" by The Dovells sold over a million copies. Kal Mann (1917-2001) and David Appell (1922-) wrote this early pop hit.

Example 21: "Bristol Stomp"

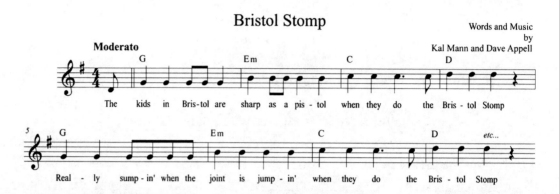

Falling Thirds, Varied: I—vi—ii—V

One chord can substitute for another if the two chords have at least two pitches in common. For example, in the key of C major the subdominant chord is F. It is composed of the three pitches, F, A, and C. The supertonic chord, Dm, is made up of the pitches, D, F, and A: the two triads share the pitches F and A, therefore, one chord can substitute for the other.

Using this concept, we can easily modify our falling thirds chord progression, I—vi—IV—V, to become I—vi—ii—V. This progression is slightly more potent than the original I—vi—IV—V because it also incorporates a root movement by fourth, ii—V. The progression of ii—V, supertonic to dominant, is very important and is found in many songs we will analyze.

"Blue Moon," (Example 22) written by composer, Richard Rogers (1902-1979) and lyricist, Lorenz Hart, (1895-1943), uses the progression I—vi—ii—V for the first six measures of each of the first two eight-measure phrases (measures one through six and nine through fourteen).

Example 22: "Blue Moon"

The progression, I—vi—ii—V, can also occur at the end of a phrase. The songwriter James Taylor (1948-) ends each verse of his song, "Carolina in My Mind," (Example 23) with these chord changes.

Example 23: "Carolina in My Mind"

RISING THIRDS: I—III⁷

In the previous progression, the I chord moves directly to vi. The tonic (I) can also progress to the submediant (vi) by moving through the submediant's dominant. In this progression, I moves to III^7, which functions as V^7 of vi. Here, vi becomes a *temporary tonic* and III^7 its dominant. In this progression, III^7 is considered a *secondary dominant*, a dominant for a temporary tonic. Using secondary dominants is a very helpful way to move to almost any chord and to prolong a phrase.

Here is how songwriters John Lennon and Paul McCartney use the progression I—III^7—vi in their song, "World Without Love." In Example 24, the tonic, C, moves to III^7 (E^7) and then to vi (Am). Note that the I—III^7—vi progression is followed immediately by a falling thirds movement. In measures three and four, vi^7 (Am^7) moves to IV (F). Here, a *passing tone* in the bass connects the two chords and provides a smooth transition. Passing tones are tones that move stepwise to embellish the movement between two chord tones.

Example 24: "World Without Love"

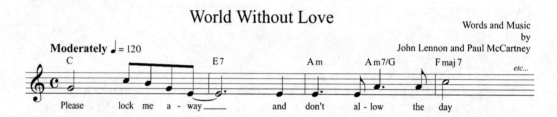

The song "All of Me," (Example 25) by Gerald Marks (1900-1997) and Seymour Simons (1896-1949), was introduced in 1931 and has become a "standard" that has been recorded many, many times.

Example 25: "All of Me"

To analyze the harmonic progression of this warhorse, I'd like to work backwards. Let's start at the end of this eight-measure phrase.

This phrase ends on a Dm chord. To arrive at the Dm, the writers precede it with its dominant-seven chord, A[7]. Working backwards again, we can now view the A[7] as the *target* chord and see that its dominant-seven chord, E[7], precedes it. Once the harmony is lifted up to E[7], it was easy to progress upwards repeatedly by fourths. Root movement by fourths is important and ubiquitous in pop music. We'll see many examples as we proceed. Let's look at another kind of upward moving root movement by third.

RISING THIRDS: I—III—IV

The long-lived hit song by George David Weiss (1921-2010) and Bob Thiele (1922-1996), "What a Wonderful World," (Example 26) begins with the chord progression I—iii—IV. Here, the goal is to move the harmony from the tonic (F) in measure one to the subdominant (B[b]) in measure two. The goal is achieved by passing through the mediant (iii).

Example 26: "What a Wonderful World"

NOTE

The term "phrase" is defined variously to mean a unit of music that is usually four to eight measures long and that expresses a more or less complete musical thought, or that which can be sung in one breath. If nothing else, music theory is imprecise.

By now, you will have noticed that the progression of the chord root often, but not always, provides the bass movement for a song.

As I have noted, sometimes composers create bass movement by moving the bass through an inverted form of a chord. In Example 27, from James Taylor's "Carolina in My Mind," the bass moves from a root position tonic chord (F) to a tonic chord in first inversion (F/A) to reach the IV chord.

Example 27: Bass Movement in "Carolina in My Mind"

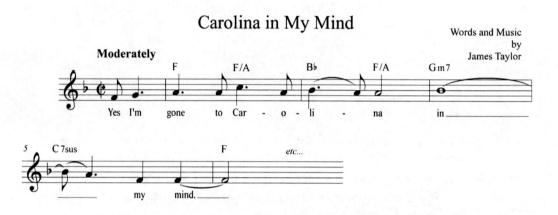

PROGRESSION BY FOURTHS: ii—V—I

Let's take another look at the progression ii—V—I, lifted from the I—vi—ii—V—I progression above. The ii—V—I progression is quite special and very often used in pop songs. Following is a song that employs this progression as a major component of its reason for being, or raison d'etre, since we're looking at a pop song from France.

Introduced in the 1946 film, *Les Portes de la Nuit*, "Autumn Leaves" began life as, "Les Feuilles Mortes." The music is by the composer Joseph Kosma (1905-1969), with the original French lyric by Jacques Prévert (1900-1977). Johnny Mercer (1909-1976) wrote the English lyric.

The first full measure of "Autumn Leaves" (Example 28) is harmonized with a two-chord (Cm^7) in $B^\flat$ major. The supertonic then moves to the dominant (F^7) in measure two, and the tonic ($B^\flat$) in measure three. Advance now to measure five. In measure five, we find an Am^7 chord that moves in measure six to a D^7, and then a Gm in measure seven. Consider for a moment that the Gm in measure seven might be the real tonic of the song (it is, by the way: this song is in G minor). If we do, then the Am^7 to D^7 to Gm can be understood as another ii—V—I progression. To be accurate about two things, this would be a minor tonic, and therefore analyzed as i. In addition, ii in G minor is not truly Am^7, it is A^{07}, but we'll talk more about minor keys a bit later…promise!

If you're counting, that's two true ii—V—I progressions, especially if we only consider the bass movement. Notice now that the bass movement is rising fourths (e.g., C to F to B^b). This progression of rising fourth motion in the progression of roots is continued as (in measure three and four) the F^7 of measure two resolves to the B^b in measure three, and then to the E^b in measure four.

Further, the E^b of measure four moves to the Am^7 of measure five, another fourth movement of roots. Then, as we've noted previously, the root of the Am^7 (A) moves up a fourth to the root of the D^7 chord (D), and then up another fourth to the G of the Gm chord. In other words, a chain of fourth progressions harmonizes the entire first eight measures of "Autumn Leaves"! Viewed another way, one can think of every third chord as a tonic; back up two chords, and see in it the root progression ii—V—I (e.g., Cm^7 – F^7 – $Bbmaj^7$, where $Bbmaj^7$ functions as the tonic).

Music theorists place special importance on the progression of harmonies that move in fourths. We'll more closely examine this progression and completely discuss what is known as the *circle of fourths* a bit later.

Example 28: "Autumn Leaves"

FALLING TO SEVEN: I—VII AND I— ♭VII

The song, "Dindi," (Example 29) by composer Antonio Carlos Jobim (1927-1944), with the English lyric by Ray Gilbert (1912-1976), and the Portuguese lyric by Aloysio de

Oliveira (1914-1995), contains a chord progression that moves from I (E$^\flat$) to $^\flat$VII (D$^\flat$) in the first two measures. The immediate effect is startling, because the harmony built on $^\flat$VII is so foreign to the tonality of the home key. Things calm down a little when the composer takes us to the temporary key of the subdominant, A$^\flat$, in measure four.

Example 29: "Dindi"

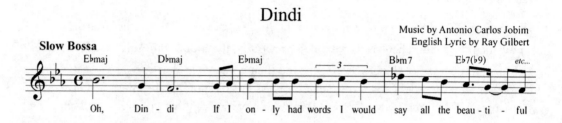

"The Days of Wine and Roses," (Example 30) written by composer Henry Mancini (1924-1994) and lyricist Johnny Mercer, was awarded an Academy Award as Best Original Song in 1962. Like "Dindi," it begins with a progression from the tonic to $^\flat$VII. However, instead of returning to the tonic (F), Mancini uses $^\flat$VII (E$^\flat$) as a passing chord in his move to the secondary dominant-seven (D^7) of ii (Gm).

Example 30: "The Days of Wine and Roses"

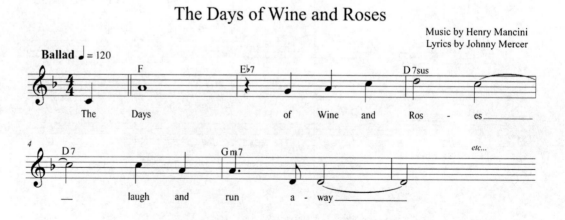

Now, we turn our attention back to John Lennon and Paul McCartney. Their song "Yesterday" (Example 31) begins on the tonic harmony (F) and, in the second measure, moves to a minor chord on the leading tone (Em). We quickly learn that Em is functioning as ii in the key of D. The third measure of the song resolves on Dm, moving first to Em^7 (ii^7) to A^7 (V^7 of Dm).

Example 31: "Yesterday"

BEGINNING ON SOMETHING OTHER THAN I

Not all songs begin on the tonic harmony. When a composer chooses to begin a song with a harmony other than the tonic, he establishes a sense of ambiguity. The listener does not know clearly from the beginning what key he is experiencing. The ambiguity about the key center creates a degree of tension that is released only when the tonic is finally sounded.

In Example 32, the standard, "Gone With the Wind" by composer, Allie Wrubel (1905-1973) and lyricist Herb Magidson (1906-1986), the tonic of E^b major is not heard until the second measure, where it is the resolution of a ii—V—I progression.

Example 32: "Gone With the Wind"

Similarly, "I Should Care," (Example 33) by Sammy Cahn (1913-1993), Alex Stordahl (1913-1963), and Paul Weston (1912-1996), begins with a ii—V—I progression that is extended by a kind of *deceptive* resolution.

A true deceptive cadence or resolution is one where V resolved to vi instead of I. In this song, V does not resolve to I in measure two; it resolves to iii as a substitute for I.

Remember that chords can substitute for one another if they share two chord tones. In this case, iii is Em (E, G, B) and I is C (C, E, G). These two chords share the pitches E and G. The ii—V—I progression is finally resolved in measure four with an *authentic cadence* from V to I.

Beginning on the supertonic and then prolonging the resolution to the tonic creates tension and ambiguity. Perhaps the composer wanted to create a sense of being unsettled to underscore the sarcasm of the lyric, "I should care, I should go around weeping."

Example 33: "I Should Care"

I Should Care

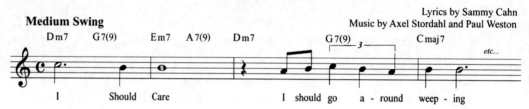

Lyrics by Sammy Cahn
Music by Axel Stordahl and Paul Weston

Harry Warren (1893-1981) and Al Dubin (1891-1945)

The great songwriting team of Harry Warren (1893-1981) and Al Dubin (1891-1945) created a similar effect with their 1934 song, "I Only Have Eyes for You" (Example 34).

It begins on the supertonic, but moves to V^7 of ii, and then back to ii, to begin a series of three iterations of ii-V. The tonic is finally sounded for the first time in measure five. By beginning on ii (Dm) and following it with the dominant of ii (A^7), Warren causes us to feel that we are hearing a song that is in the key of D minor. This sense is unfulfilled when he returns us to Dm and then follows up with several playings of Dm to G^7, ii—V—ii—V—ii—V—I (finally!). The sense of mystery and wonder that is expressed in the lyrics is underscored by music that is not obviously grounded in a sense of key.

Example 34: "I Only Have Eyes for You"

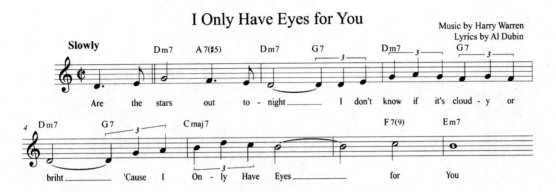

Songs with Few Changes

Many, many songs whose melodies are supported by only a few chords have become very successful. They derive their momentum, drive and interest from something other than a series of interesting chord changes. It might be a compelling lyric, a driving bassline, or, in the case of a record production, a particularly compelling rhythm track and sensational performance by a lead vocalist. Whatever it is, these songs have become commercially successful even though they possess very little harmonic variety.

"Chain of Fools," by Don Covay (1938-) with a hit record released by Aretha Franklin, is composed of one chord: Cm. The hit song, "Be Thankful for What You Got," with a hit record made by its writer, William DeVaughn (1947-), has only two chords, $F^{\#}m$ and Em. Finally, the song, "American Woman," by the Canadian group, The Guess Who, is built around one chord, an E chord. Released with great success in 1970, the song was an improvised jam by the band's members, Randy Bachman, Garry Peterson and Jim Kale with lead singer, Burton Cummings, ad-libbing the lyrics. The compelling lyric and Burton Cummings powerful delivery, along with a propulsive rhythm powered by a driving bass riff, helped make this song a commercially successful record.

EXERCISES

Example:

Given:

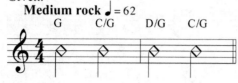

Compose a new melody for each of the chord patterns provided. Be sure to keep in mind the tempo (indicated as beats per minute) and the style. Your final melody should fit exactly the style and tempo indicated.

One method for creating a new melody over given chord changes is to create a simplified melody using just chord tones. Do this in your first draft.

First draft

In the first draft, write a very simple melody that is composed of chord tones only.

Second draft

In the second draft, elaborate your melody by adding passing tones.

Exercise #1

Given:

First draft:

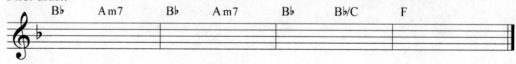

Second draft:

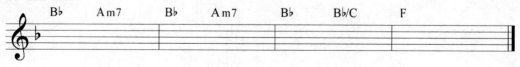

Exercise #2

Given:

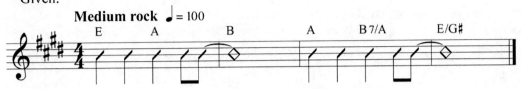

First draft:

Second draft:

Exercise #3

Given:

First draft:

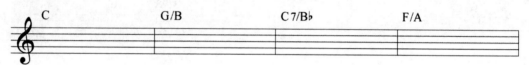

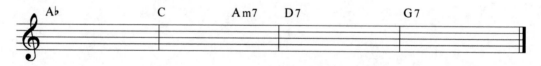

Second draft:

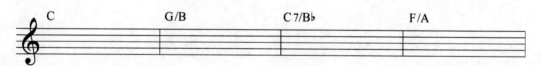

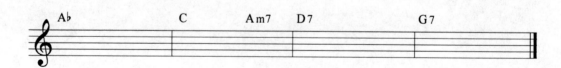

Exercise #4

Given:

First draft:

Second draft:

Exercise #5

Given:

Med. Pop ♩ = 104

First draft:

Second draft:

Exercise #6

Given:

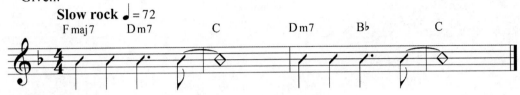

First draft:

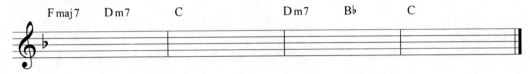

Second draft:

CHAPTER TWO

SONGS IN SINGLE PERIOD FORM

In chapter one, I introduced what I believe are some of the essentials of music theory one must know to compose songs in today's popular styles. I also provided many of the chord progressions one finds in pop music.

In this chapter, I will demonstrate how songwriters put those theory fundamentals to work to create great songs. Along the way, I will also introduce additional music theory material, including a few new scales, chords and some terminology.

My method for demonstrating how to compose good pop tunes will be to analyze some standard songs from the pop literature. I will also analyze a few songs of my composing. Through dissection of well-crafted songs, I believe that one can learn what to do and what to avoid doing.

Some will question my choices of songs for analysis, especially since many of these include very old songs or songs that are not well known. Here is the thing: Well-done is well-done. Our analysis will revolve around musical form, the construction of the melody, the lyrics and the harmony. These aspects of composing change little from generation to generation. What changes are the way these musical features are presented in the musical arrangement, and if a song is recorded, in the production.

I begin our journey of musical and lyrical analysis with a thoughtful look at the Christian hymn, "Amazing Grace."

SINGLE PERIOD FORM

The sixteen measures that make up "Amazing Grace" can be considered a *musical period* or simply, a period. In pop-style songs, as in longer compositions, a period is defined as two musical phrases that work together to convey to the listener a complete musical statement. The first phrase of a period concludes without ending, creating in the listener an expectation that there will be more music to come. The second phrase ends conclusively. It is this sense of incompleteness followed by completeness that composers rely on to keep listeners engaged. The composer, through the *cadence* expresses completeness or incompleteness in music. A cadence is a harmonic or melodic movement that creates in the listener a sense of arrival, resolution and repose.

The culmination of a cadence is the chord of resolution or in a melodic cadence, the note of resolution. If a cadence resolves on a harmony that is not the tonic it is experienced by the listener as sounding incomplete and requiring more musical elaboration. Cadences that resolve on the tonic are heard as complete. They are heard as especially strong and final if scale step one is in the melody.

Example 35 demonstrates two cadences, a *perfect authentic cadence* and a *half cadence*. The perfect authentic cadence features melodic motion that resolves on scale degree one and a harmonic movement that progresses to the dominant and resolves on the tonic.

Example 35: V to I CADENCE

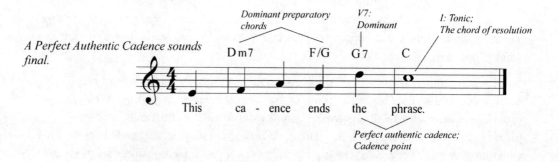

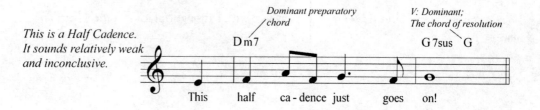

In the perfect authentic cadence example, the entire two measures, plus the pick-up note, E, can be construed as a cadence. The Dm7 and the F/G chords serve as *dominant preparatory chords*, as they help establish the harmonic move to the dominant chord, G^7. The C chord is the *chord of resolution*, the goal of the harmonic motion. Melodically, there is also a *melodic cadence* as the pitch, B, resolves to the pitch, C. Note that the conclusion of this melodic phrase coincides with the conclusion of the lyrical phrase.

The half cadence resolves melodically on scale step five and harmonically on the dominant leaving the listener hanging in suspense and wanting to hear more.

Musical periods in many pop songs model their construction after the periods found in the music of the late 18th and 19th century. They are often composed of two smaller sections of music called *phrases*.

The musical phrases are generally complimentary in that they work well together and lead from the first phrase to the second to form a unified whole. The complimentary phrases of a period are sometimes called an *antecedent* and a *consequent*, and are often described as a question and answer.

In the concert music of the Classical period, the periods were often sixteen measures long, made up of two eight-measure phrases. The phrases are, in turn, often made up of shorter phrases or *sub-phrases* of four measures each. We will soon discover as we analyze other songs that periods can be joined together to form longer compositions.

Single Period Form is sometimes called by other names, including *strophic form*. A strophic song is one where all the lyrics are sung to a single melody. In strophic-style lyric setting, the melody is repeated with very little variation form verse to verse.

ANALYSIS OF SONGS

In dissecting the music of any song, we will want to determine the song's *musical form*, *harmonic motion*, *melodic shape* (or *contour*) and *melodic rhythm*. In our analysis of the song's lyrics, we will ascertain the song's *lyrical form*, *prosody* and *rhyme scheme*

"Amazing Grace," is, according to the American music historian, Gilbert Chase, "without a doubt the most famous of all the folk hymns." It is estimated that "Amazing Grace" is performed about 10,000 times each year and has been recorded hundreds of times. The lyrics and the melody began as separate works that were joined together several years after they were created and after each had enjoyed years of celebrity and use.

The melody and harmony of "Amazing Grace" began life as a tune called, "New Britain." In 1831 "New Britain" appeared in a chapter called the *Virginia Harmony* and was attributed to a man named James Carrell. Some, however, attribute an earlier version of the tune to Charles Spilman and Benjamin Shaw who wrote the anthology, *Columbia*

Harmony (also called the *Pilgrim's Musical Companion*), published in 1829. It is, in fact, unclear who composed "New Britain." It is possible that Mr. Carrel and the others did not compose the tune, that they were simply transcribing a *folk melody* whose authorship was undetermined.

Folk tunes, folk melodies, folk hymns—any music described as being folk is a piece whose composer and or lyricist are unknown and lost to time.

Folk music is that which has come down to us through the years as part of an oral tradition passed from one generation to the next. Because the composer or composers of "New Britain" are not known, the credits on the song are most often listed as "Anonymous."

The English poet and clergyman, John Newton (1725-1807), wrote the text of "Amazing Grace" and included them, without musical accompaniment, as part of a sermon he delivered at the church in England where he preached. The Reverend John Newton's poem was first published in 1779 in a collection called *Olney Hymns*. Written by Newton and his writing partner, William Cowper, it included several hymns and the text to a sermon by Newton entitled, "Faith's Review and Expectation." The sermon is the text of the song that became known for its opening line: "Amazing Grace."

When Newton introduced his now-famous words, he might have given "Amazing Grace" a choral recitation in a tradition called *lining out*, where the leader read a line and the congregation repeated it in unison or where the leader sang a line that was then repeated.

John Newton's sermon we know as "Amazing Grace" became very popular. Over the years, musicians made many settings of Reverend Newton's text by accompanying the words John Newton wrote with existing songs and newly composed songs. Someone put Newton's text together with the "New Britain" tune sometime during the 1830's. This successful pairing has endured ever since.

FORM, KEY AND METER

Good songs, like all successful works of art (and indeed, most utilitarian things in our lives, too), are constructed according to some formal plan. A shirt is recognized as a shirt only if it has certain criteria: some accommodation for the arms, the neck and some covering of most or the entire torso. At its most basic level, the formal plan for a song is words that express a singular thought that are sung to a tune (music) with a beginning, middle and end.

This basic description does not provide enough information to help significantly an aspiring songwriter craft a memorable song. It will be more helpful to scrutinize what is the precise structure for several successful songs.

In analyzing a song, we answer several questions and describe how the separate parts are presented. These questions include: How long is each section? How many sections are there? In what order do the sections appear? Are they repeated, and if so, are they varied as they recur? How is the melody harmonized? What is the form of the lyric?

ANALYSIS OF "AMAZING GRACE"

We will begin our song analysis of "Amazing Grace" with general observations and move to the details. As we proceed with our analysis, I will define some new terms. Going forward, you will see that these terms are used all the time. My goal is to provide you the tools you will need to analyze any song.

A REASON TO ANALYZE

Why bother to create a detailed analysis of music? Why is it important to know what other songwriters do? Other than pure academic curiosity, the rationale for in-depth musical analysis might seem murky. However, knowing what great songwriters did to create their great songs will percolate through your songwriting in quiet and hard to discern ways. My hope is that you will be influenced in your decision-making by modeling your choices after those made by the writers of the songs you analyzed, that you would incorporate into your songwriting the techniques you observe in the songwriting of others. This is a good thing!

THE METER OF "AMAZING GRACE"

"Amazing Grace" is composed in 3/4 meter. Music occurs in time that is measured by beats, an even succession of metrical pulses, like the sound that is made when one marches. Beats are grouped in patterns of strong and weak pulses. Most songs are characterized by the regular recurrence of these patterns. This is the song's *meter*. In music notation, one complete occurrence of one of these patterns is called a *measure*. The meter of a song or a section of a song is indicated by a fractional number called a *time signature* or *meter signature* that is placed at the beginning of the composition or section thereof. The denominator of the time signature indicates the basic note value of the meter (what note value receives the basic beat of the piece). The numerator indicates the number of note values in a measure (how many beats are found in each measure).

In Example 36, we see the 3/4 meter signature of "Amazing Grace" which indicates that the quarter note receives the beat (or basic pulse) and that there are three beats in each measure.

Musicians count the beats of the measure, often subdividing them so they can keep the pulse even, and to know where they are in the music. For instance, in 3/4 one will count, "one, two, three" or "one and two and three and." In 3/4 meter, we will experience a strong pulse on "one" followed by two weak pulses on "two" and "three."

Example 36: Time Signature, Counting, and Tempo Indication

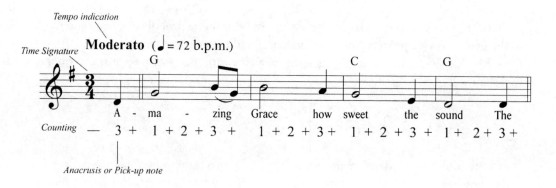

There are several other time signatures that are commonly used in *pop music*. These include: 2/2, 2/4, 4/4, 5/4, 6/8, 7/8, 9/8 and 12/8.

TEMPO

Tempo is the rate of speed at which the beats of a piece of music proceed. Tempo is indicated by some direction at the beginning of a piece or section of a piece of music. In older music, words like slowly, *moderato* or *andante* would be used to communicate a relative tempo, but supplied the performer with little specificity about how the speed of

the piece. Contemporary music is frequently more precise, using a formula like ♩ = 72 b.p.m., the abbreviation for beats per minute to indicate the actual speed at which the composer wants the composition to be realized. Example 36 and Example 55 demonstrate two ways to correctly indicate tempo sheet music.

Metrical Accents in Music

The first beat of the measure (the downbeat) of all commonly used meters, 2/4, 3/4, 4/4, 5/8, 6/8, receives the primary accent. The downbeat is more heavily accented than any other beat in the measure no matter what the time signature. In compound meters such as 4/4, 5/8 and 6/8, a secondary accent is experienced. In 4/4, the secondary accent is on the third beat; in 5/8, it is on either the third or the fourth beat; in 6/8, the secondary accent is on the fourth beat.

Why is it Important to Know about Musical Accents?

Language and music share some characteristics. For songwriters, one of the most important of these is that they are both sounds that occur in time and in rhythm. As we speak, we place more or less stress on one syllable or another. The stresses in our speech correlate to the accents experienced in music, so when setting lyrics to music it is important that the musical accents line up with the lyrical accents. If the accents do not correspond, the listener may not easily perceive the words and the meaning of the lyrics might be lost. Lyrics that flow in a rhythmically natural way will always be more easily heard and remembered.

"Amazing Grace" is Composed of Sixteen Full Measures, Plus a Pick-up Note.

Pick-up note: Also called an *anacrusis*, a pick-up note is one or more notes that occur before the first metrically strong beat of a *musical phrase*. In "Amazing Grace," the pick-up note is sung to the "A" of the first "A-maz-ing."

A musical phrase is a unit of artistic expression that is usually made up of sub-phrases and always ends with a harmonic and melodic *cadence*. A cadence is a harmonic progression that accompanies a melodic line that creates in the listener a sense of repose. We will see that some cadences require no further resolution and sound final. Some cadences create only a pause in the flow of music and allow for the music to proceed to another phrase.

The Phrase Structure of "Amazing Grace"

A phrase in music is analogous to a clause in language. Phrases are almost always part of a larger section of music called a *period*. Songs in popular style are most often composed using phrases with an even number of measures. It is common for songs to have four-measure sub-phrases and for those sub-phrases to be grouped together, to form eight measure phrases. Of course, most rules are to be broken. John Lennon and Paul McCartney created the most recorded song in popular music, "Yesterday." Its first two phrases are seven measures long!

"Amazing Grace" is very regular in its formal phrasal structure. It is composed of two eight-measure phrases. Each phrase is made up of two four-measure sub-phrases. Together, the two eight-measure phrases form one sixteen-measure period. See Example 37.

Labeling Conventions in Musical Analysis

All the components of a song can be labeled to aid in our analysis and discussion. I use these labeling conventions:

Table 5: Labeling Conventions

Component	Label Type	Example
Periods	roman numerals	I, II, III, etc…
Phrases	capital letters	A, B, C, etc…
Sub-phrases	lowercase letters	a, b, c, etc…
Phrases that recur with variation	parenthesis	B (like A), and so on.
Sub-phrases that recur with variation	superscript	a^2, a^3 and so on.

Example 37: Complete Periods with Phrases and Sub-Phrases Marked

ESTABLISHING THE KEY

The melody of the first phrase (A) begins with an anacrusis on scale degree five. The first strong beat of the melody of the A-phrase is a tonic, scale degree one, that is supported by a tonic (I chord) harmony.

By sounding the dominant on the pick-up note and the tonic on the first strong beat of the melody, the anonymous composer of "New Britain" firmly establishes the key center of the song. Our example in this case is in the key of C-major.

The establishment of a key is important. Key centers are hinted at by the playing of the dominant and tonic in the melody, but are firmly established by the composer since he harmonized those melody notes with a dominant (V chord) and tonic (I chord).

Establishing the key early in a song is important. In doing so, the composer essentially declared that he would follow several well-established conventions. Most of these revolve around how he would choose melody notes and how he would choose to harmonize those melodies. Establishing a key and adhering to the tenants of the tonal system is important in popular music. I have introduced some of these rules and conventions in Chapter One. I will add more as we move forward.

THE SHAPE OF A MELODY: MELODIC CONTOUR

All melodies have a shape; this is its *melodic contour*. A simple drawing using arches can represent the melodic contour of a song.

Let's look back to Example 37. The melody of the first eight-measure phrase (A) ends in measure eight on scale degree five. This is the climax of the first full phrase. The melody is supported here by a dominant harmony (the V chord). Both the melody, by ending on scale degree five, and the harmony, by ending on the dominant, creates a sense of the song is not yet over. There needs to be a concluding phrase to bring the listener back to a resting point on the tonic in the melody and the harmony. A musical phrase that moves harmonically from tonic to dominant is called an *opening phrase*. The tension that is created in the listener by this musical inconclusiveness is important and encourages the listener to continue listening.

The melody of the second eight-measure phrase (B) begins on scale degree five, supported by a tonic harmony. This phrase also begins with an anacrusis on scale degree three on the word, "I" of the phrase, "I once was lost…"

The second phrase begins on a tonic harmony and ends on a tonic harmony. A phrase that begins and ends on a tonic harmony is a circular phrase. In "Amazing Grace/New Britain," the B-phrase serves to complete the A-phrase. The sense of completion I observe here is the result of both the harmonic motion and the melodic motion. Since the first phrase begins on a tonic chord and ends in measure eight on a dominant seventh chord, it engenders a sense that it is incomplete. As listeners, we are up in the air. The second phrase brings us back down to Earth by resolving the harmonic progression in measure sixteen to a tonic chord and ending the melody there on a tonic.

In our example the melody begins on a low G (on the pick-up note), moves through the first phrase to a high G (scale step five in measure eight) and gradually, during the second phrase, resolves back down to a C (the tonic pitch in measure sixteen).

The first four-measure sub-phrase (a^1) returns in slightly varied form as the concluding four measures of the B-phrase. The reiteration of the opening material provides a "bookend" for the other musical sections and helps to unify the song. The last sub-phrase is an almost exact repeat of a^1, so I label it as "a^3." This labeling indicates that this sub-phrase a^3 is composed of the same music, but that it is slightly varied. By repeating a varied version of sub-phrase a^1, and ending it with a very final-sounding cadence theorist call a *perfect authentic cadence*, the composer creates a palpable sense of completeness. The listener has heard the opening sub-phrase end up in the air. Now they hear the end of the story.

PERFECT AUTHENTIC CADENCE

A perfect authentic cadence consists of a V to I chord progression where the last melody note is a tonic. It is arguably the most final-sounding cadence in tonal music.

THE EMOTIONAL ARCH OF "AMAZING GRACE"

Aware of these observations, one could logically state that the hymn "Amazing Grace" (in terms of its melody and harmony) begins calmly, increases in perceived tension, and then resolves back to a place of rest during each verse, melodically, harmonically and lyrically.

GRAPHING THE MELODIC CONTOUR

If one were to draw an arch to graphically represent the direction of the melody, one would have the apex of the arch correspond with the word "me" in the first line of the text: "Amazing Grace, How sweet the sound that saved a wretch like me!" From that point in the song, having created a heightened sense of tension, the composer gradually brings the listener to a point of relative rest at the end of the B-phrase during the singing of the lyric, "I once was lost, but now am found; Was blind, but now I see." Example 38 illustrates the melodic contour just described.

It is very common for songs to engender in the listener a sense of building tension that is released by the end of the song.

Example 38: Melodic Contour

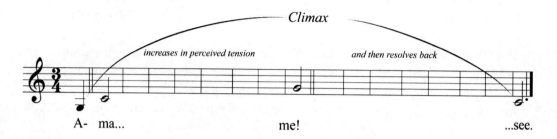

MELODIC DEVELOPMENT

When a composer concocts a great melodic hook, she usually repeats it over and again. However, exact repetition causes boredom so when a composer repeats a hook, she often, but not always, varies it. Creating changes to a melody over a musical span of time is called *development*.

The composer of "New Britain/Amazing Grace" uses this concept of development (or varied repetition) with great results (Example 39). For instance, the opening of the second phrase (measure nine with its pick-up) contains the same music as the opening of the first phrase (measure one with its pick-up). However, the music is varied: It is *transposed* up a third. In other sections, the composer of "New Britain" repeats musical material almost exactly.

The first sub-phrase is exactly the same as the second sub-phrase, except that the first phrase ends on scale step five down the octave. The second phrase ends on scale step five up the octave. In our example, sub-phrase one ends on a low G. Sub-phrase two ends on a high G.

The second four-measure sub-phrase, a², is like a. Recall that I indicate the similarity of the sub-phrases with my labeling. Again, the sub-phrases begin the same, but end differently. The first two measures of the sub-phrases are exactly the same. Only the third and fourth measures are different.

The last sub-phrase, a³, is an almost exact repeat of the first sub-phrase, a¹. Again, a³ begins exactly like the first sub-phrase, but ends just a little differently.

Play through the four sub-phrases of "Amazing Grace" as they are listed in the next example. Play one, pause for a few seconds and then play the next. Notice the similarities between the four sub-phrases. Notice that sub-phrase a³ begins exactly like sub-phrase a¹, but ends differently. Sub-phrase a³ ends with a very final sounding cadence in both the melody and the accompanying chord.

While the development of the melody in this song is fairly modest, it does clearly demonstrate a technique you can employ readily in your writing. We will see the technique of melodic development used often by successful songwriters in the following chapters.

In the next chapter, I will introduce another song form that mimics the formal structure of the sub-phrases of "Amazing Grace:" a¹, a², b, a³. Called *Twentieth Century Bar Form*, it was the most popular form of the Twentieth Century. It is the form of the majority of songs in the standard literature of American and European popular music.

Example 39: Four Sub-Phrases a¹, a², b and a³

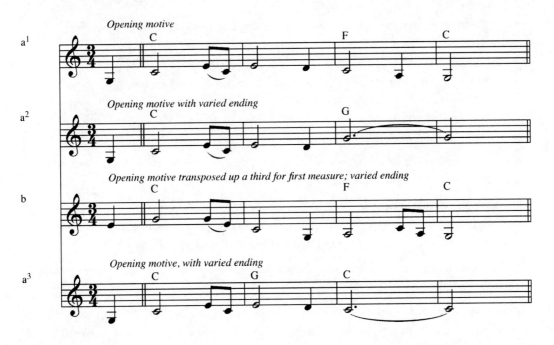

Melodic Hooks

All successful songs have *lyrical hooks* and *melodic hooks*. The main lyrical hook and the main melodic hook usually happen together. The melodic hook accompanies the lyrical hook.

The term hook, as used in pop music (especially recordings), refers to any short lyrical phrase (as short as a word or two) or any short melodic fragment. A hook in a musical arrangement for a pop record production might be:

- a distinctive lick played by the rhythm section, like the opening of the Dave Brubeck Quartet's 1959 recording of "Take Five" written by Paul Desmond (1924-1977),
- a distinctive instrumental lick that recurs often, like the ascending six-note line played by the electric guitar in the Temptations' 1964 recording of "My Girl" written by Smokey Robinson (1940-), and Ronald White (1939-1995), or
- an unusual instrumental sound, like Anthony Jackson's bass guitar (modified with a phase shifter by recording engineer, Joseph Tarsia) on the 1973 recording of "For the Love of Money" written by Kenneth Gamble (1943-), Leon Huff (1942-), and Anthony Jackson (1952-).

A musical hook could be an unusual vocal sound, like Frankie Valli's voice on any of the records he made with his band, the Four Seasons.

Hooks, whether instrumental or lyrical serve to draw listeners in to a recording. Hooks help the listener remember a song and act as memory triggers. One needs to hear but a little bit of a musical hook to be reminded of the entire song or recording.

As I explained in Chapter One, music theorists call the principal melodic hook of a song (or longer composition) a motive.

The principal musical motive of "Amazing Grace" is its opening lick, that which accompanies the words, "A-ma-zing Grace." Like all motives, this one is rhythmically impressive. It has a precise and distinctive rhythm (a quarter note up beat followed by a half note and two eighth notes). Like many motives, it outlines the underlying harmony. The initial statement of the principal motive of "Amazing Grace" sounds all the pitches of the tonic harmony (the I chord). As demonstrated in Example 39, the opening motive in "Amazing Grace" recurs four times in slight variation, occurring on different pitches or being completed with slight, but important, changes.

MOTIVES UNIFY SONGS

Melodic motives, and their modified repetitions, unify songs. A listener is introduced to a melodic lick, hears it again and again (accepting its slight variation as they listen), and, as is the case in "Amazing Grace," hears it repeated at the end of the song with a strong, final cadence. The listener learns the motive, learns to trust the songwriter as he repeats the motive (without being boring, because he has varied it a little), and then accepts the song or part of the song as complete when the songwriter repeats it one last time, ending it with a sound the listener knows means, "the end."

MELODIC AND HARMONIC COMPONENTS OF "AMAZING GRACE"

The melody of "Amazing Grace" uses only five pitch-classes. In the key of C-major these are, C, D, E, G and A. This set of pitches is special and, when arranged within an octave, form the *pentatonic scale*.

PENTATONIC SCALE

The name *pentatonic* is derived from the Greek words for five ("pente"), and tone ("tonic"). There are several pentatonic scales. The most common is the *major pentatonic scale*. The pitch arrangement of the major pentatonic scale is the same as the black keys of the piano beginning with G-flat. There is a whole step between the first and second, and second and third degrees of the scale, a minor third between scale steps three and four, and a whole step between the fourth and fifth degrees. The several other pentatonic scales will be presented subsequently.

One can think of forming pentatonic scales in a number of ways. One is to take the first five pitch-classes of the *circle of fifths* (C, G, D, A and E) and arrange them within one octave. Another is to think of a pentatonic scale as a major scale without the fourth or seventh degree.

Pentatonic scales are found in the music of many folk traditions, from the British Isles to all of Europe, from Asia to Africa to America. Theorists suggest that pentatonic scales are so ubiquitous because they lack dissonance. There are no minor seconds or sevenths and no *tritones* (the interval of an augmented fourth or diminished fifth, the span of three whole steps). These intervals are heard as dissonant in all cultures.

As with other scales, pentatonic scales can be transposed. They can be built up beginning on any pitch by maintaining the scale formula of intervals between pitches. The formula for the pentatonic scale is whole step, whole step, minor third (one and a half steps), whole step. In theory, one can extract five different arrangements of the intervals in the pentatonic formula (Example 40).

In practice, musicians usually think of a *major pentatonic* and a *minor pentatonic*. The major pentatonic begins with the pattern as presented, where the first three scale steps span a major third. The minor pentatonic begins with the leap of the minor third, followed by the three pitches spanning the major third.

Example 40: Common Pentatonic Scales

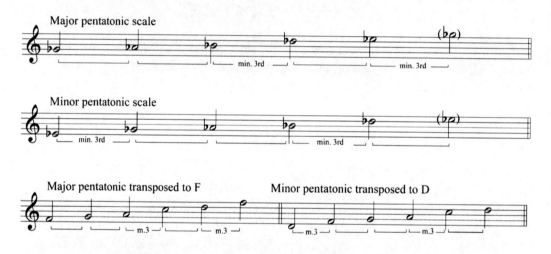

HARMONIZATION

Because "Amazing Grace" is a tonal song in a major key, it can be harmonized satisfactorily using the three primary chords or pillar chords: Tonic, subdominant, and dominant (I, IV and V). This means that an accompaniment can be created for this melody that uses only the primary chords of the major scale, for instance a C-major triad, F-major triad and G-major triad in the key of C major. Tonal music is composed using major, minor and pentatonic scales and employs a set of conventions, like creating a hierarchy of pitches and their corresponding harmonies to create in the listener a sense of movement, direction, arrival and repose. Other systems of musical organization, like the twelve-tone (also called dodecaphonic or atonal system), or the quartal system are, in my experience, not used in creating pop-style songs. Some successful pop songs have been written using a modal system of organization. I will discuss modal songs in a subsequent chapter.

The ii chord (the supertonic), the iii chord (the mediant) and the vi chord (the *submediant*) are thought of as secondary chords. The vii chord (the leading tone triad) requires special care (and, perhaps, feeding) and is reserved for special functions, for instance as a substitute for the dominant chord under certain circumstances. (As such, it is presented in first inversion, where the chord third appears in the bass.) A chart of diatonic chords is presented in Chapter One.

Re-harmonization

Songs are often re-harmonized by arrangers desirous of creating an original version of a well-known song. This process involves the replacement of certain chords with others that the arranger deems to be more appropriate for the assignment at hand. The subject of *chord substitution* is complicated in its depth of possibilities. In brief, as mentioned previously, one chord can often substitute for another if both chords share at lease two chord tones. This method is not foolproof since it does not take into consideration the movement of the chord roots and how that motion sounds against the melody. I encourage the reader to listen to my choral arrangement of "Amazing Grace" (*Amazing Grace: A Choral Fantasy*), to hear at least one arranger's take on how an old "chestnut" can be souped up.

I will provide more specific information on chord substitutions (that is what some musicians call re-harmonization) in the next chapter. This is an important topic. The mastery of it will provide you with more interesting and attractive songs.

The Lyrics of "Amazing Grace"

"Amazing Grace" has five or six verses of lyrics (depending on the edition one uses) that are each sung to the same melody. The melody remains constant while the lyrics change from verse to verse. Songs that employ this technique of lyric setting are said to be, *strophic*. Single Period songs are always strophic.

"Amazing Grace" is a Strophic Song

In *strophic songs*, the melody stays the same while the lyrics change with each new verse. The strophes of the poetical lyrics in "Amazing Grace" each follow an identical rhyme scheme. This is consistent with strophic poems. We will later see that lyrics and poems share many characteristics, but that lyrics are not always poems. Remember, though, that the lyrics of "Amazing Grace" were originally a poem and that they were later wedded to the melody of the tune, "New Britain."

Strophic songs are especially useful in telling a story or, as is the case with hymns, educating illiterate congregants about the Bible.

Lyrical Hooks

Like instrumental hooks, lyrical hooks draw listeners in and help them remember a song. Lyrical hooks are typically short phrases of words that are accompanied by the main melodic motive. The lyrical hook of "Amazing Grace" is its title. As is the case with many strophic songs, the title of this song appears at the very beginning of the song. The primacy of this placement supplies its import. Because it comes first, it is remembered.

The Title in the Hook

Lyrical hooks in successful songs always include the song's title. (Actually, there may be a song whose title does not appear in the lyrics, but I cannot remember it. Ergo the problem with not including the title in the lyrics.)

Rhyming in Lyrics

Lyrics are poetic, but not poems. They share some characteristics, like rhythm, meter, and rhyming. However, lyrics are generally more like the sentiments on a greeting card than they are like long, scholarly poems. Even though the text of "Amazing Grace" is a poem, it was performed aloud as part of another presentation. Its contents are, therefore, in simple language.

Since songs that are performed are ephemeral, they occur in the performance and then vanish into the ether; their lyrical content must be succinct. Most poems are for reading. The content of a poem is often more dense than that of most songs. The structure of a poem is often more complicated, too. The reader of a poem can usually return to reread a line or a stanza without much trouble. Song lyrics, when performed, must be remembered since they might not be heard again very soon, or ever.

Lyrics do not have to rhyme, but it just helps if they do. Rhymes help anchor a lyric and, along with the rhythm of the melodic motive, help the listener hear and remember what is being sung.

RHYME SCHEME OF "AMAZING GRACE"

The lyrics of "Amazing Grace" follow a *rhyme scheme* of A B A B. Each four-measure phrase of the melody ends with a lyric that is rhymed. In the first verse, the rhyming words are; sound and found; see and me. The rhyme scheme stays consistent throughout the song's six verses.

Table 6: Rhyme Scheme of Amazing Grace

Verse One	(Rhyme scheme)
Amazing Grace, how sweet the sound	A
That saved a wretch like me!	B
I once was lost but now am found;	A
Was blind, but now I see.	B

I have now written (and you have read) quite a lot about just sixteen measures of music! Determining what makes a great song work takes some significant detective work, but you will find doing that work to be extremely helpful to your songwriting.

Many helpful things can be gleaned from this kind of sleuthing. One thing that might now be apparent is that successful compositions can be built up of a small amount of musical material that is repeated and varied. During the course of our analysis of other songs you will observe this trait many times. It is a truism that music will likely not be well remembered if it is not repeated. But, it will be boring if it is repeated without variation.

Some Critical Comments about "Amazing Grace"

A few additional thoughts about the great hymn, "Amazing Grace," are appropriate at this point. In spite of its tremendous popularity and phenomenal longevity, the song does present some features that, I think, do not demonstrate great tunesmithing. My criticism is in the setting of the lyrical hook, the title, "Amazing Grace," and the setting of other words or syllables to more than one note in the melody.

There are a few methods available to songwriters to emphasize syllables. Important syllables to be accented can be set to music that is also accented, they can be set to longer notes, they can occur at a high point in the melody, at the end of a melodic phrase or after a dramatic pause. English (and some other languages) is a stress-timed language, where stresses, pauses, the length of a syllable and the relative pitch used to speak the syllable indicate the *prosody* of the oral presentation of the language. For the songwriter this means that, absent some special reason, it is always preferable to have the important, and accented syllables of the lyric set in such a manner that they are sung to notes that are similarly stressed. In plain language: The important words need to be placed on important notes.

The First Issue

The setting of the second syllable, "ma-" in the word, "A-ma-zing."

We do usually accent the second syllable of "amazing," so setting the second syllable on the accented beat of the measure seems like good thinking. However, this first note of the first full measure of the tune is also a long note, therefore adding extra weight to this note and the syllable that accompanies it. This seems overdone to me. To draw out the syllable, "ma" momentarily distorts the perceptibility of the word. One could argue that such a "mispronunciation" creates memorability, and perhaps it does.

In Example 41 I present the present, traditional setting of the lyrics for the opening measures of "Amazing Grace" alongside a new setting. My proposed new setting accommodates what I believe is a more common pronunciation of the word, "Amazing."

Example 41: Proposed New Setting of Lyrics for "Amazing Grace"

THE SECOND ISSUE

It takes too long to get to the third syllable, "-zing" in the word, "A-ma-zing."

One usually pronounces the word, "Amazing" in such a manner that all three syllables receive the same duration. The lengthened second syllable, sung at the moderately slow *tempo* in which the hymn is usually performed, makes it take too long to get to the last syllable. This extra pause causes momentary confusion in the mind of the listener because this is not the way one normally *hears* the word said. The modification of the opening music presented in Example 41 also provides a shorter singing of the second syllable of "Amazing."

THE THIRD ISSUE

The last syllable of the first word is sung over the span of two shorter notes, providing it extra and undue weight.

Stretching out a syllable over two or more melody notes draws attention to the melody and away from the words, thereby obscuring the meaning of the syllable and consequently the word. The two eighth notes that accompany the syllable, "-zing" in the word, "a-ma-zing" are an example of *melismatic writing*. I am stretching the meaning of the word, *melisma*, just a bit since the precise definition is a single syllable accompanied by group of more than a few notes. My argument stands: In pop-style songs, singing any syllable to more than one note makes it harder for the listener to discern what is being sung because it distracts the listener's attention to the performer's technique, taking the attention off the significance of the text. The modification of the opening music presented in Example 41 provides a suggested single-note singing of the final syllable of the word, "Amazing."

Of course, criticism of almost anything so tremendous popularity and phenomenally long-lived places the critic in a precarious position. My criticism is borne of a desire to illustrate how not to set lyrics and to introduce the notion that songs can become popular for many reasons, not only because they adhere to some certain set of guidelines, alas—even mine!

OTHER SONGS IN SINGLE PERIOD FORM

Many other songs have been created in this form. Here are just a few:

- "Mack the Knife" ("The Ballad of Mack the Knife" or "Die Moritat von Mackie Messer") Music: Kurt Weill (1900-1950) and Lyrics: Bertolt Brecht (1898-1956)
- "Old MacDonald Had a Farm" (traditional nursery rhyme; Roud Folk Song Index number 745)
- "By the Time I Get to Phoenix" Words and Music by Jimmy Webb (1946-). This song adds a change to the form in the last verse, but the song is essentially in Single Period Form.
- "The Wreck of the Edmund Fitzgerald" Words and Music by Gordon Lightfoot (1938-). This song is interesting because it incorporates in its single period two five-measure phrases in 6/8 meter followed by two four-measure phrases.
- "I Walk the Line" Words and Music by Johnny Cash (1932-2003). Mr. Cash includes the title hook at the end of each verse and, in performances, followed each sixteen-measure period with a few measures of instrumental interlude.
- "House of the Rising Sun", Huddie William Ledbetter (January 20, 1888 – December 6, 1949)

SINGLE PERIOD FORM: THE BLUES

Songs in *Blues Form* are also composed of a single short period, usually of twelve measures. Like "Amazing Grace" and "Mack the Knife" and other Single Period Form songs, blues songs are strophic, composed of two interrelated phrases, and easily harmonized using the primary chords.

The phrases of Blues Form songs are not balanced.

Sometimes the basic Blues Form has been successfully adapted for use in a rock tune. These blues-rock hybrids are most often composed of an eight- or sixteen-measure period that often contains two unbalanced phrases.

TWELVE-BAR BLUES

The vernacular term that musicians use for *measures* is *bars*. Thus, it is common for musicians to refer to songs in the most common blues form as "twelve-bar blues."

THE BLUES AS A PRODUCT OF THE AMERICAN MUSICAL MELTING POT

The blues is a musical genre that was developed in America during the nineteenth century. It combines African musical performance styles and the music of the European-American Protestant Church.

The blues genre was significantly marked by the experiences of enslaved African-Americans and their freed descendants as they struggled for peace and equality in the United States after the Civil War and into the 20th century. That the blues began in the "Deep South" of the United States—South Carolina, Mississippi, Florida (especially the Panhandle and north central Florida), Alabama, Georgia, Louisiana and East Texas—in the late 19th century is no mere coincidence. These states were slow in recognizing the equality of African-Americans, an unfortunate remnant of their membership in the Confederate States of America and the philosophy it espoused. Ironically, during this same time, many blacks were also exposed to and welcomed into the integrated camp meeting worship services of itinerate preachers.

The blues form exhibits influences from many sources, including simple rhymed ballads, field hollers, work songs, shouts, Protestant hymns and white and black spirituals.

Spirituals are one of the most important antecedents of the blues. Spirituals include both revival and camp meeting songs and date back to the early part of the 19th century. A major, non-denominational religious movement called the Second Great Awakening swept across the United States during the 1800's after originating in Britain. The camp revival meetings of the Second Great Awakening became an important vehicle for Protestant sects, especially Methodists and Baptists, to bring the unreligious back to God.

Worshipers traveled great distances to camp out in remote locations to hear the teachings of itinerate preachers. Camp revival meetings were not only non-denominational; they were also for the most part open to all comers. It was common for African-Americans to attended camp meetings with European-Americans. The revival meetings of the Second Great Awakening became a true musical melting pot that white European folk and formal music intermingled with black performance style. Indeed, most African-American spirituals were created in a white folk music style.

The folk music traditions of European-Americans and African-Americans share many elements. For instance, both are largely based on pentatonic scales. This is not surprising.

As we have learned, the pentatonic scale is found in the folk music of people the world over. Many of the pentatonic and major scale melodies of African-American spirituals are borrowed from European-American and British (especially Scottish and Irish) folk music.

Blues singers, like the folk singers of the Balkans and southern Europe, sometimes sing with a non-tempered scale. In both traditions, some pitches are intoned in a variable manner. For instance, blues singing is often typified by the inclusion of *blue notes*—the purposeful singing a bit flat of scale degrees three and seven.

CALL-AND-RESPONSE

The practice of *call-and-response* is a compositional and performance technique where in one artist or group of performers presents a musical fragment that will be either replicated or responded to by a second artist or group or performers. The call-and-response technique is found in the musical traditions of many peoples. In the classical music of North India, this kind of performing is known as *sawaal-javaab*, literally, question-answer. The call-and-response pattern can also be found in the work songs of Europe. For instance, the anthropologist, Alan Lomax, working in southern Italy in the early 1950s documented the songs of olive pickers. His recordings provide evidence of a leader who sings a line that is followed by a response sung by the workers.

Another common call-and-response practice, begun in the mid-17th century, was the lining out of psalms. In congregations that could not read, a leader would intone or line out the psalm text one line at a time alternating with the congregation's singing of that same line. The lines were sung to familiar melodies often ornamented and varied with passing notes. This was the technique that Reverend John Newton used to introduce "Amazing Grace" to his congregants.

Similar to these several examples, blues songs and other song forms provide many cases where a phrase of music and a phrase of lyric (the question or call) are answered by a subsequent musical and lyrical phrase (the answer or response). Blues Form songs, and other kinds of songs, often employ the call-and-response pattern similar to the lining-out technique.

THE EARLIEST BLUES

The spirituals of Black Americans were not only sung in worship, but also as work songs. Eventually, the spiritual genre evolved over time and was adapted to become a vehicle for secular topics. Accompanied by an African-American style of performance—adding grace notes, turns, melisma and purposely singing scale steps three and seven "blue"—spirituals provided the beginning point for the blues.

The earliest documented use of the term "blues" is in a composition by W.C. Handy called, "Memphis Blues," written in 1909. A recording of the piece made in 1914 by the Victor Military Band reveals that, after a four-measure introduction, Handy employs a varied version of the basic twelve-measure blues chord pattern as his starting point. From there, Handy unfolds a multi-sectional piece in the style of the popular marches of the day. (The period from just after the American Civil War through about 1940 was a time of great popularity for military-style marching music and bands.) The "Dallas Blues" by songwriter Hart Wand was the first copyright registered using the term "blues." This was in 1912.

Musical Form: Twelve-Bar Blues

Blues songs are generally created in a 4/4 meter with four beats in each measure and the quarter note receiving the basic pulse. The essential blues form is characterized by a single twelve-measure period that is composed of two unbalanced phrases. The first phrase, A, is eight measures long. The second phrase, B, is four measures. The A-phrase is a phrase group made up of two sub-phrases: a^1 and a^2.

The melodic and lyrical hook is presented in the first sub-phrase. The melodic hook and its accompanying lyric is repeated in the second sub-phrase (a^2). The melody of a^1 is supported by the tonic harmony, often with an added minor seventh, yielding a non-functional dominant seventh chord on the tonic (I^7). The second sub-phrase, a^2, is harmonized with the subdominant harmony, also with an added minor seventh, yielding a non-functional dominant seventh chord on the subdominant (IV^7).

Non-Functional Dominant Seventh Chords as Color Chords in Blues

In most traditional European contexts, the interval of a minor seventh is added to the dominant chord to form a V^7 at cadence points, for instance at the end of a period when V^7 resolves to the tonic. Example 42 shows the harmonic accompaniment for the standard, twelve-bar blues. Note that the interval of the minor seventh is regularly added above the bass of the tonic and subdominant triads to provide *color*. The tonic seven (I^7) and the subdominant seven (IV^7) are considered non-functional since they are not used at cadence points. The seven chord built on the dominant (V^7) is also non-functional when, in measure nine in the blues progression, it moves back to the subdominant. This, too, is not a cadence point since it provides no sense of finality. The V^7 chord in measure twelve *is* functional because it does occur at a cadence point. In measure twelve, the V^7 chord serves as a vehicle for allowing the repeat of the song, returning it back to the beginning of the period for another playing with a new verse.

Example 42: Twelve-Bar Blues Chord Progression in C-Major

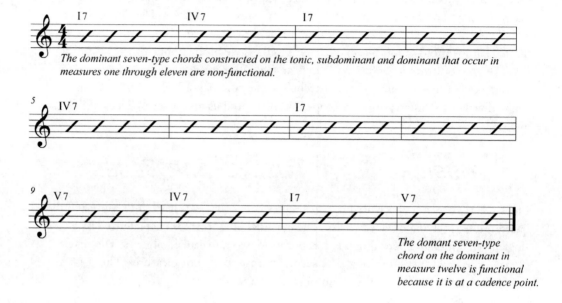

The dominant seven-type chords constructed on the tonic, subdominant and dominant that occur in measures one through eleven are non-functional.

The domant seven-type chord on the dominant in measure twelve is functional because it is at a cadence point.

BLUES MELODY

Blues melodies normally include elements of the *blues scale* (also called the *jazz scale*), a modified form of the major scale, that incorporate several *color tones* or *blue notes*. Blue notes or color tones are defined variously as pitches that are sung or played slightly flat or, as we will define them (relative to the major diatonic scale performed), with scale steps three, five and seven replaced with flatted notes. In the key of C-major, E becomes E-flat, G becomes G-flat and B becomes B-flat. The natural form of the pitch can be found in blues tunes alongside the altered scale steps. (See examples of the blues scales and the transcription of "Backwater Blues.")

THE BLUES SCALES

There are several forms of the blues scale commonly used in American music. These include a six-note blues scale in two species (or versions), a seven-note blues scale, an eight-note blues scale and a nine-note blues scale.

The most complicated form, the nine-note scale, incorporates elements of the major diatonic scale, the natural minor scale and the *Lydian mode*. (The Lydian mode or scale can be thought of as a major scale where the fourth degree is raised one half step. More information about the Lydian mode can be found in the Appendix.)

Example 43: The Five Blues Scales

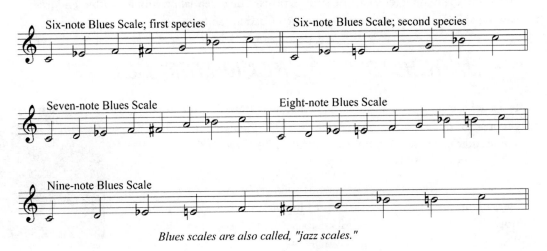

Blues scales are also called, "jazz scales."

Lyrics in Blues Tunes

Lyrical topics expressed in the blues spoke of the African-American condition after the Civil War. Blues lyrics often include tales of economic hardship, mistreatment, crime and punishment, violence, sex, drinking, natural disaster and traveling on the railroads.

The lyrics of songs in blues form follow one of two regular patterns. Generally, a blues song will start with a line of lyric that presents a proposition or conveys the condition of the singer. That lyrical message is sung to a melody undergirded by the harmonies of the first four measures.

The lyric is repeated exactly during the next four measures if it fits over the chords for the second four-measure phrase. If the melody does not fit well exactly as is, it will be varied slightly to fit the new harmony. In a second type of blues lyric pattern, the second lyrical phrase can amplify the story, add to the proposition or otherwise elaborate the storyteller's situation.

The last lyrical phrase coincides with the last four-measure harmonic phrase. The lyrics for the last phrase sum up and provide a conclusion for the verse. They supply a resolution to the issues introduced in the first two lyrical phrases.

Strophic

Blues songs, like other Single Period songs, are strophic: The lyrics change from verse to verse and are sung over an accompaniment that remains essentially unchanged as the verses unfold. Creative musicians elaborate, decorate and otherwise vary their playing to create and maintain interest as the song evolves. The essential harmonic rhythm endures and the chords change at the measures prescribed in the template.

ANALYSIS OF "BACKWATER BLUES"

It is not clear who created the song, "Backwater Blues." It is credited variously to both Bessie Smith (April 15, 1894 – September 26, 1937) and Huddie William Ledbetter (January 20, 1888 – December 6, 1949), also known as "Lead Belly."

Huddie William Ledbetter (January 20, 1888 – December 6, 1949), also known as "Lead Belly."

The song is a prototypical blues tune. It follows the twelve-measure blues chord progression typical of the blues and the lyrics follow the story development pattern described above. Like all twelve-bar blues, "Backwater Blues" is strophic (Example 44).

Example 44: "Backwater Blues"

Words & Music by Huddie
Ledbetter; Published by Folkways
Music Pubishing, Inc. © 1962 Oak
Publishing, Inc.

Transcribed and
Editedd by LAd

Backwater Blues

Huddie Ledbetter

Moderato ($\quarternote$ = c. 108)

It rained five days and the sky turned dark as night—

It rained five days and the

sky turned dark as night—— There was

trou-ble tak-ing place in the low—— land that night.——

2.
I woke up this morning, wouldn't even
   get out of my door,
I woke up this morning, wouldn't even
   get out of my door,
Enough trouble to make a poor girl
   wonder where she gonna go.

3.
It thundered and it lightened and the
   winds began to blow,
It thundered and it lightened and the
   winds began to blow,
There was a thousand women didn't
   have no place to go

4.
I went out to the lonesome, high old
   lonesome hill,
I went out to the lonesome, high old
   lonesome hill,
I looked down on the old house where
   I used to live.

HARMONIC PROGRESSION

"Backwater Blues" begins with an anacrusis, an "E" that accompanies the word "It" in the opening phrase: "It rained all day and the sky turned dark as night."

The melody in the first two full measures of the first sub-phrase (a¹) outlines a second species six-note blues scale. Like most all twelve-bar blues, the melody is repeated during the second four-measure sub-phrase (a²). It is accompanied in the second sub-phrase with the subdominant harmony (a IV⁷ chord).

In this song, the tonic, subdominant and dominant chords are all altered to include the minor seventh above the root (forming non-functional dominant seventh chords on all three primary chords). "Backwater Blues" follows the standard blues chord progression. The melody of the song flows logically from these chords with both featuring the use a lowered scale step seven (Example 45). Note also the characteristic use of the lowered third, as an antecedent to the raised (major) third, as in measures one and five.

Example 45: Opening Of "Backwater Blues" Showing the Flat Seventh

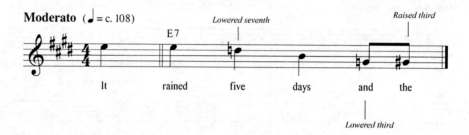

In blues form the first two sub-phrases (a¹) and (a²) can be taken together to form an *antecedent phrase group*. If the second four-measure sub-phrase were deleted one would have a simple Single Period song (Example 46).

Example 46: Eight Measures of "Backwater" Without A²

The last sub-phrase (b) provides a musical and lyrical answer, a *consequent phrase group*, to the opening phrase group. As in the sixteen-measure Single Period songs (like "Amazing Grace"); the A-phrase (the A-phrase group in the case of blues form) poses a musical question that is answered in the consequent phrase, B.

LYRICS

The lyrics of "Backwater Blues" create a similar antecedent and consequent arrangement. A basic condition is presented: "It rained all day, and the sky turned dark as night." A rough circumstance that so impressed the storyteller that he or she is obliged to repeat the first telling for emphasis. Then, in the B-phrase the consequence of the awful circumstance announced in the first phrase group is delivered: "There was trouble taking place in the lowland that night."

The pattern of antecedent and consequent, condition and response, is repeated in each subsequent verse. With each new verse, the basic chord pattern of the accompaniment remains the same.

In his lyrics for "Backwater Blues," (Example 47) Ledbetter does not use rhyme as a unifying technique. He does frequently repeat words from the end of one line to the next. He does rhyme, though. For instance at the end of verse 2, "go" matches the rhymes of the next verse where it rhymes with "blow." The word "go" then recurs at the conclusion of verse 3.

I speculate that Ledbetter's lyrics were mostly improvised around the central core of an idea (in this case a flood) and that it was more important to him to relate the story's message and emotions than to display his mastery of a fancy lyric writing technique.

Example 47: Lyrics for "Backwater Blues"

Backwater Blues, Lyrics by Huddie William Ledbetter

Verse 1

It rained all day, and the sky turned dark as night.
It rained all day, and the sky turned dark as night.
There was trouble taking place in the lowland that night.

Verse 2

I woke up this morning, wouldn't even get out of my door.
I woke up this morning, wouldn't even get out of my door.
Enough trouble to make a poor girl wonder where she gonna go.

Verse 3

It thundered and it lightened and the winds began to blow.
It thundered and it lightened and the winds began to blow.
There was a thousand women didn't have no place to go.

MUSICAL ARRANGEMENT AND RECORD PRODUCTION OF SINGLE PERIOD SONGS

From a practical standpoint, all Single Period songs present a challenge and an opportunity for musical arrangers and producers. They are so very simple that they are very, very memorable. At the same time, unvaried repetition in music can foster boredom. Musicians solve the issue of potential boredom by creating musical arrangements that feature subtle changes in harmonization, instrumentation and key center. The novelty of the new—an added instrument or voice, an added countermelody, a transposition to a new key, the inclusion of an instrumental solo or interlude—can help overcome the built-in challenges of this simple song form.

A quick listen to the classic recordings of "Mack the Knife" by Bobby Darin (or the wonderfully humorous live recording of the song by Ella Fitzgerald), or the hit recording of "Sunny" by Bobby Hebb will provide some ideas about how these simple song forms can be arranged and produced.

Released in 1966, Bobby Hebb's recording of his song, "Sunny" became an enormous success, selling millions of copies and being rerecorded by other performers more than one hundred times. Broadcast Music Incorporated (BMI) has included "Sunny" as number twenty-five in its list of *Top 100 Songs of the Century*.

"Sunny" is typical of the sixteen-measure Single Period song, providing all of the benefits and all the issues. The composer, arranger and guitarist, Joe Renzetti arranged the music for the 1966 recording. In his classic arrangement, Renzetti uses a rhythm section that included guitars, electric bass, drum kit, vibraphone, a small horn section and a couple female back-up singers.

Following is a graphic summary of Joe Renzetti's arrangement for "Sunny." (Example 48) In it, I have noted where throughout the five verses of the original recording Renzetti adds new musical elements. Adding these subtle, effective changes in the arrangement provides just enough novelty to keep the arrangement fresh and the song interesting. I am quite sure that Renzetti's great arrangement helped to establish Hebb's fine song as the classic it has become.

Example 48: Joe Renzetti's arrangement for the song, "Sunny."

Sunny

Words & Music by Bobby Hebb
Arranged by Joe Renzetti

SIXTEEN-MEASURE BLUES SONG FORM

The classic progression of the twelve-bar blues has sometimes been modified with very successful results. The hit song, "Watermelon Man," written in 1962 by the pianist/composer, Herbie Hancock (1940-), extends the basic twelve-bar blues pattern at measure eleven by inserting the V to IV progression two additional times. In Hancock's song, this repetition helps to build the drama, and is climaxed with a break on beat one of measure fourteen. Other variations can be found in the literature that expands the basic twelve-bar pattern at other spots. These are valid and valuable. Other sixteen-measure blues songs include, "I'm Your Hoochie Coochie Man," written by Willie Dixon (1916-1992), and "Let's Dance" written by Jim Lee and released by Chris Montez in 1962. The chord patterns for both songs are included in Example 49.

"Let's Dance," like "Watermelon Man," adds an additional V to IV progression at measure eleven, but then returns to the tonic chord for four measures. As is the case with "Watermelon Man," "Let's Dance" does not add a dominant chord in measure sixteen. There is no preparation for the return to the beginning. It just happens!

"I'm Your Hoochie Coochie Man" is also a One Period, sixteen-bar blues, but it has some additional features that make it stand out. There is a pick-up measure that leads into the first phrase. The first eight-measure phrase is in a "stop chorus-style." In a "stop chorus," the rhythm section plays only the first beat of each measure while someone solos. In "Hoochie Coochie Man," it is the singer who is the soloist. All eight measures of the first phrase are accompanied by a tonic seven chord. The second eight-measure phrase moves to a subdominant seven chord as it follows the chord pattern of the last eight measures of the standard twelve-bar blues.

Example 49: Variations on the Blues Chord Progression In Sixteen-Bar Blues

This example demonstrates the flexibility of the 12-bar blues. Each songwriter began with the basic 12-bar blues chord pattern and then added four measures to suit his particular needs. Songwriters are always playing with the rules! Often, to great advantage.

Exercises

Exercise #1

A. Compose an eight-measure openng phrase that contains two four-measure sub-phrases. (Have the phrase end on the dominant.) Compose in a key that will make this phrase easy for you to sing. Use "Amazing Grace" as your model.

B. In composing your phrase, begin with a one- or two-syllable word that is set to the initial melody of your phrase.

C. Create additional lyrics for the eight-measure phrase you wrote. Have the additional lyrics provide additional context and more information.

Exercise #2

Using a story from the current news as your lyrical starting point, create a
blues tune that clearly presents a prdicament in the first phrase group. In your lyrics, have the
B-phraseprovide a consequence. Explain what happened because of the predicament, for
instance.

Blues tempo

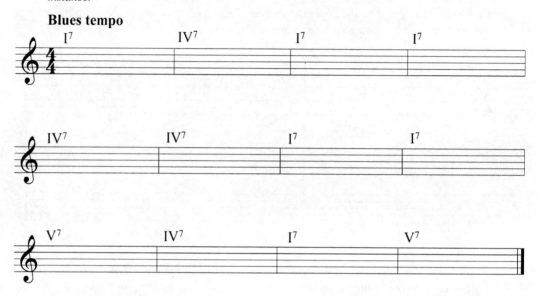

Exercise #3

Using the information I provided about the way motives are repeated and varied in
"Amazing Grace" as a starting point, find other instances where the songwriter has
repeated the principal motive in some kind of variation.

Exercise #4

Compose an opening motive for the first sub-phrase of a new blues tune.
Using the concept of repetition with variation, create a second sub-phrase that repeats
the motive with variations that take into account the change of harmony (the move to

IV^7*) required in the blues form.*

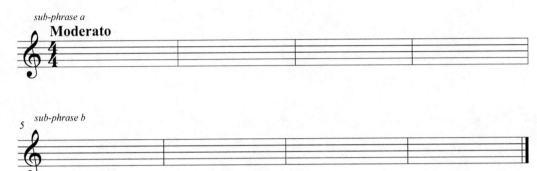

Exercise #5

Create a harmonic and phrasal analysis for "Mack the Knife" and "House of the Rising Sun."

Exercise #6

Create additional lyrics for "Mack the Knife" and "House of the Rising Sun" maintaining the same melodic rhythm, form and rhyme scheme.

CHAPTER THREE

INTRODUCTION TO DOUBLE PERIOD FORM

I demonstrated in the previous chapter that a successful song could be composed of a single musical period. Single musical periods can also be joined with other periods to form multi-period songs. In fact, most songs in the popular literature are composed of two or more interdependent musical periods.

Songs composed of two periods are called *Double Period* songs and are said to be in *Binary Form*. The two periods of the Double Period song are interdependent; they work together to convey a unified musical expression.

THREE TYPES OF BINARY SONGS FORM

Binary songs are found in three different configurations. They are the Verse/Chorus song, the Twentieth Century Bar Form song, and the *Pop Song Binary Form* song. All three forms are well represented in the popular literature of the nineteenth, twentieth and twenty-first centuries.

Verse/Chorus Songs

The Verse/Chorus form has endured for generations.

Examples of successful verse/chorus songs include: "Oh! Susanna" and "Old Folks at Home" by Stephen Foster (1826-1864), "'O sole mio" by Giovanni Capurro (1859-1920) and Eduardo di Capua (1865-1917), "Lucy in the Sky with Diamonds" from the 1960s by Lennon and McCartney, "Superstition" by Stevie Wonder (1950-) in the 1970s, "Every Breath I Take" by Sting (1951-) from 1983 and from the twenty-first century, and "Let's Get This Party Started," by Linda Perry (1965-).

Each of these songs contains two periods, a verse and a chorus.

The Verse Period and the Chorus Period

A *chorus* in popular music refers to a period that recurs, sung each time with the same lyrics. The chorus almost always contains the title of the song. The chorus of a song us usually repeated many times in a typical presentation and for this and some other reasons I will describe, is the part that people most often remember.

In popular music the term *verse* is used to describe the words and music of the other period of the verse/chorus song. The verse period usually precedes the chorus.

The principal purpose of the music and lyrics of the verse period is to prepare the listener for and lead them to the memorable music and lyrics of the song's chorus.

The verse is where the songwriter establishes the premise of the song, provides context, and otherwise entices the listener to want to hear the chorus. All sections of great songs can and usually do contain melodic, lyrical and accompaniment hooks, but verses are generally less filled with memorable motives and lyrics then are choruses.

Verses will usually conclude on a dominant chord of whatever key the chorus is in. Ending on the dominant helps provide an easyrmonic transition to the chorus.

Verses Are Strophic

Verses of pop songs are strophic. The same (or nearly the same) music is used for the singing of each new stanza of lyric. The lyrics of the verse introduce the story of the song. They are expository and usually provide a lot of information about the short drama that is to unfold in the course of the song. With each new verse more details unfold.

LYRICS OF THE CHORUS

The chorus delivers the consequence for the story or issue presented in the verse. Certain things have transpired in the verse and as a result the spokesperson (the singer/narrator) says these other things in the chorus. Songwriters usually provide in the chorus a succinct and memorable lyrical hook that sums up the story. The lyrical hook almost always becomes the song's title. A memorable melodic hook always accompanies the lyrical hook. A great song that follows this general lyric and melodic scheme is Stevie Wonder's classic tune, "I Just Called To Say I Love You." (Example 50)

ANALYSIS OF
"I JUST CALLED TO SAY I LOVE YOU"

Stevie Wonder begins verse one by clearly establishing that today is just "another ordinary day." The motivation for the call is not yet stated.

Example 50: Lyrics from "I Just Called To Say I Love You"

I Just Called To Say I Love You (Words & Music by Stevie Wonder, 1984)

Verse One

No new years day to celebrate
No chocolate covered candy hearts to give away
No first of spring, no song to sing
In fact here's just another ordinary day

By the time Wonder leads us through the end of the second verse, we are quite ready to learn what is going on. Why is he (the spokesperson/singer) bothering to try to convince us that there is nothing important about today? Who cares if there is no rain or that it is not a Saturday in June? And, why are you speaking to us in riddles? What are these three words that you feel compelled to utter?

I Just Called To Say I Love You

Verse Two

No April rain, no flowers bloom
No wedding Saturday within the month of June
But what it is, is something true
Made up of these three words that I must say to you

Finally, in the chorus we the listeners learn that "what it is." What is special is that the spokesperson is in love. Further, we discover that he is not speaking to us; we are overhearing a conversation that the spokesperson is having with the person on the other end of a phone line. The singular reason for the singer's phone call we discover in the chorus is to express love for the person on the other end of the line. The song's premise is established, the little bit of confusion about precisely what was spoken of in the verses is quelled and in the chorus a clear declaration of affection is made to the call's recipient.

Chorus

> I just called to say I love you
> I just called to say how much I care
> I just called to say I love you
> And I mean it from the bottom of my heart

This song's lyrics are succinct, sweet and very successful. "I Just Called to Say I Love You" was one of Stevie Wonder's most commercially successful songs. His recording achieved a number one position on the *Billboard* "Hot 100", "Adult Contemporary" and "R & B" charts, won a Golden Globe and Academy Award for Best Original Song (it was included in the 1984 comedy, *The Woman in Red*) and received three Grammy® nominations.

The simple Verse/Chorus form is profoundly efficient. In just two periods the songwriter weaves a story and, in one period, repeats a title many times to establish it in the listener's memory. There are many fine examples of this unadulterated Verse/Chorus form, but there are also many more cases of the Verse/Chorus form in slightly modified versions.

PLACEMENT OF THE TITLE HOOK

The lyrical and melodic hook may appear at the beginning, the middle or the end of the chorus (or in more than one place, including in the verses). The chorus period of the song provides the "take away" for the listener. It is the section most listeners will remember, the part of a song that average listeners will sing to you if you ask how a song goes.

In the Stevie Wonder song, the lyrical hook and its accompanying melodic hook appears at the beginning of the chorus and then again in the middle of the chorus. This placement is very typical and can be seen in many Verse/Chorus songs.

Of course, there are always successful exceptions to almost every rule about songwriting. For instance, in the song "The Gambler," written by Donald Schlitz (1952-) and made famous by Kenny Rogers in his wonderful 1978 recording, the song's title appears in various places throughout this story song, but not in any of the spots typical of Verse/Chorus songs (Example 51).

Lyrical Analysis of "The Gambler"

Example 51: Lyrics from "The Gambler"

The Gambler (Words & Music by Donald Schlitz)

Verse One

On a warm summer's evenin' on a train bound for nowhere
I met up with the gambler, we were both too tired to sleep
So we took turns a starin' out the window at the darkness
'Til boredom overtook us and he began to speak

Verse Two

He said, "Son, I've made a life, out of readin' people's faces
And knowin' what their cards were by the way they held their eyes
So if you don't mind my sayin', I can see you're out of aces
For a taste of your whiskey I'll give you some advice"

Verse Three

So I handed him my bottle and he drank down my last swallow
Then he bummed a cigarette and asked me for a light
And the night got deathly quiet and his face lost all expression
Said, "If you're gonna play the game, boy, you gotta learn to play it right"

Chorus

You got to know when to hold 'em, know when to fold 'em
Know when to walk away and know when to run
You never count your money when you're sittin' at the table
There'll be time enough for countin' when the dealing's done
Every gambler knows that the secret to survivin'
Is knowin' what to throw away and knowing what to keep
'Cause every hand's a winner and every hand's a loser
And the best that you can hope for is to die in your sleep

The spokesperson in this song is a storyteller, a narrator. Through the narrator/singer the songwriter Donald Schlitz provides a story so compelling and memorable that he has no need to sing the song's title. Another songwriter might have named the philosopher-gambler and sung that name over and again in the chorus, but that would have cheapened the song significantly. Of course, Kenny Rogers' excellent performance and Larry Butler's great production help to keep the listener wanting more.

The combined talents of Schlitz, Rodgers and Butler created a recording so memorable that it flew to the top of the record charts and became a touchstone of country pop. The song, though, with its powerful message and hooky, memorable lines is the essential element in the mix of ingredients that made the recording a hit.

Interestingly, it takes one minute and ten seconds for the original recording to get to the chorus. This, too, breaks the record producer's understanding that one must get to the chorus in sixty seconds or less.

THE PERIODS OF A BINARY FORM SONG ARE BALANCED AND WORK TOGETHER

"The Gambler" breaks another rule. Usually, periods of a Verse/Chorus song are balanced, meaning that they are the same length in measures. In "The Gambler," the first verse is one and a half times as long as the chorus is.

Most often, the periods of a Verse/Chorus song are eight or sixteen measures long, but lengths can vary. Most popular songs in Verse/Chorus form are written in 4/4 meter; however, songs in 3/4 and 12/8 are not uncommon.

...BY ANY OTHER NAME

Over the years, in different regions, and in different generations song choruses have been called by other names. You might hear persons refer to this period as *the refrain*, *the hook*, *the hammer*, *the sing-along* or *the channel*.

VARIATIONS

The Verse/Chorus song form is extremely resilient. As I have demonstrated, Verse/Chorus songs can be very successful when presented in their simplest form, but many songwriters choose to modify the form by including additional sections or by rearranging the order in which the periods are presented.

REVERSE ORDERING OF PERIODS

Although it is very common for Verse/Chorus songs to be performed with the verse sung first, this is not always the case. Sometimes songwriters and arrangers present their songs with the chorus sung first.

In the original 1964-recorded performance of the song, "How Sweet It Is (To Be Loved By You)" by Marvin Gaye and the James Taylor version of the song form 1975, the chorus period of the song precedes the verse period. The lyrical hook, "How Sweet It Is," is presented at the beginning of the chorus and therefore the beginning of the song. In reality, it is the only lyric of the chorus!

Written by the great songwriting team of Eddie Holland (1939-), Lamont Dozier (1941-) and Brian Holland (1941-), "How Sweet It Is" has some other features worth noting.

FURTHER ANALYSIS OF "HOW SWEET IT IS"

The title of this great hit song grows out of a colloquial expression. The practice of creating a song's title out of a commonly used phrase is noteworthy because it is so very effective and done so often. "You Only Live Once," "For Once in My Life," "Solid as a Rock," "Diamonds Are a Girls Best Friend," "For All We Know," "Play It Again," "That's How We Roll," "Shake It Off" and of course, "9 to 5" are all illustrations of song titles that evolved from a colloquial expression.

The harmonic progression of "How Sweet It Is" (Example 52) is also interesting. The song begins on the subdominant ($IV^{\Delta 7}$), moves to the dominant (V^7; Bm^7 and Am^7 are passing and inconsequential), and then to the tonic. The entire opening of the song (the Chorus) can be seen as a IV-V-I progression.

Beginning on the subdominant, or chord any other than the tonic, creates a sense of forward movement because as listeners we want to have the harmony find its way back to the tonic. The song does find its way back to I.

NOTE:

The Melody of "How Sweet It Is" is composed using the pentatonic collection.

Example 52: Partial Phrasal Analysis of "How Sweet It Is"

How Sweet It Is (To Be Loved By You)

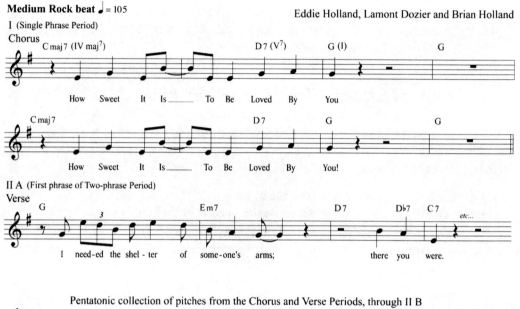

Pentatonic collection of pitches from the Chorus and Verse Periods, through II B

Example 53: Melodic Analysis is Phrase IIB of "How Sweet It Is"

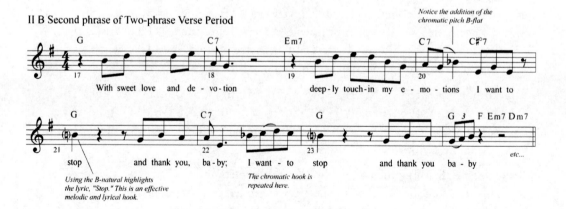

In the second period, the harmony progresses from I to V and then, using the blues chord progression as their model, Holland, Dozier and Holland end the first three sub-phrases on the subdominant-seven. The move from V⁷ to IV⁷ at the end of each sub-phrases mimics the progression found in the standard blues. The chord progression at measure eight of the second phrase of period II provides a re-transition to C-major for a repeat of the Chorus by reintroducing the F-natural (in the F-major and D-minor chords). The C-major harmony in the first measure and a half of the Chorus is the *key of the moment*, a harmony that temporarily functions as the tonic. The sense of C- is quickly defeated when on the third beat of measure two a D⁷ is introduced, leading the melody, harmony and the listener back to the home key of G-major. Many songwriters display a preoccupation with the subdominant as a target harmony in their writing.

VERSE/CHORUS COMPOSED OF TWO BLUES PERIODS

Let us look now at another successful Verse/Chorus song that provides a different set of idiosyncrasies. First, the writers were able to compose "At the Hop" by stringing together two twelve-bar blues periods. Next, the song's title does not appear in the chorus, but does appear prominently in the verse.

Artie Singer (1919-2008), John Madara (1936-) and David White (1939-) wrote "At the Hop." It was first released on record in 1958 and became a top-selling hit record in a version by Danny and the Juniors. It was covered by the band, Sha Na Na in the 1969 Woodstock Festival and featured in the film, *American Graffiti* in 1973.

"At the Hop" is composed of two twelve-bar blues periods. The first twelve-bar blues period serves as the verse, the second as the song's chorus. Interestingly, both sections include some form of the title; but curiously, the precise title does not appear in the chorus. It is placed squarely in the verse. The chorus includes only a variation of the title, but the title never appears in-full in the chorus, proving indeed that all rules are to be broken.

Example 54: Phrasal Analysis of "At the Hop"

At the Hop

Note that blues form consists of only one phrase and that phrase is also the entirety of the blue form's single period. I have therefore not marked that single phrase, A, just as in the analysis of the blues tune, "Backwater Blues" I did not indicate the single period, I.

In the analysis of "At the Hop" I have indicated the two distinct and interdependant periods (I and I) and have indicated the sub-phrases, a, a¹ and so on. I have not indicated the blues form's single phrase. It is understood.

I have labeled the first full period as the verse because it is strophic. The second full period has a single lyric and that is invariable. The phrase, "Let's Go to the Hop" recurs in this period many times without change. The songwriting team of Singer, Madara and White chose to call the song, "At the Hop" because of the prominence given to this line in the verses. They could have named it "Let's Go to the Hop" and been similarly successful.

The two most common variants of the Verse/Chorus song form are the Verse/Chorus song with a bridge and the Verse/Chorus song with a *pre-chorus*. Often both added sections are found in one song and sometimes other elements might be varied.

VERSE/CHORUS SONG WITH BRIDGE

Sometimes songwriters add a *bridge* between repetitions of the chorus (Example 55). Doing so provides variety and, especially, relief from the monotony that could result from several successive hearings of even a very interesting chorus period. Musical bridges are generally inconsequential phrases that are placed between two more significant sections of music. Bridges usually do not include musical or lyrical material that is highly developed or that adds significantly to the plot of the song.

Bridges are usually in stylistic contrast to the verse and chorus periods. For instance, if the chorus populates the melody with long notes, then the melody of the bridge might feature notes of short duration yielding a rapid rhythm. On the other hand, if the range of the verse and chorus is large the bridge might have a smaller compass. Often the bridge will start in a key center other than the key of the chorus and verse. If the chorus is in C-major, the bridge might be in A-minor; if the chorus is in E-flat major, the bridge might be in A-flat major. A change of key center is not mandatory, however, as we shall see in the example below.

Like the harmony of the verses, the harmony of the bridge must lead the listener's ear back to the chorus. Bridges will usually end on a dominant chord of the key of the next chorus.

Example 55: "You've Got a Friend" Verse/Chorus With Bridge

You've Got a Friend

Words and Music by
Carole King

© 1971 COLGEMS-EMI, INC.

The great American songwriter, Carole King (1942-) wrote, "You've Got a Friend" in 1971. It was simultaneously released on her album, *Tapestry* and James Taylor's album *Mud Slide Slim*. Both records topped the *Billboard* charts. Taylor and King won Grammy® Awards for their individual recordings of the same song: Taylor for "Best Male Pop Vocal Performance" and King for "Song of the Year."

Analysis of Verse/Chorus Song with Bridge: "You've Got a Friend"

"You've Got a Friend" begins in the key of F#-minor and resolves in measure seven and eight to A-major, the relative major. The second eight-measure phrase of the verse period hovers between F#-minor and A-major, finally ending on the dominant of A-major (E) to prepare for the chorus period in A-major. The verse period is balanced and it consists of two eight-measure phrases. The phrases differ, though, and are not a simple repeated single phrase.

Likewise, the chorus period is composed of two eight-measure phrases (Example 56). The entirety of the chorus is in A-major, ending in the first playing on the dominant of F#-minor so to return to the temporary key of the verse opening.

The bridge is begins in the temporary key center of D-major and flows through a ten-measure single phrase period back to the dominant of A-major, the key of the chorus. This allows for an easy return to the chorus.

Melodically, the bridge of the song encompasses a smaller range, from A3 to A4 than does the verse and chorus. They traverse a range from A3 up to C#4. The rhythm of the melody in the bridge is also considerably different from that of the chorus. The melodic rhythm of the chorus is a little different, too. In the chorus, the melodic rhythm is somewhat haltering, with much open space in the way of long rests. The melody features a set of pick-up notes that lead to a long note on the downbeat of the following measure.

Example 56: Measures 1 - 4 of the Chorus from "You've Got a Friend"

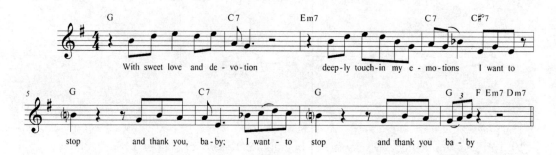

Other Verse/Chorus songs that include a bridge include: "Can't Stop" written by Flea (1962-), J.A. Frusciante (1970-), A. Kiedis (1962-), and C. Smith (1961-); and "Fix You" written by members of the band Coldplay.

Verse/Chorus with a Pre-chorus

Many Verse/Chorus songs add a short phrase of new musical and lyrical material that is placed just prior to the chorus. This is a *pre-chorus*. It further prepares the listener to hear the important message of the chorus. It heightens the anticipated arrival of the chorus.

Let's return to "How Sweet It Is" for a look at how the writer prepares the listeners for the chorus.

Holland, Dozier and Holland add a second phrase to the verse that serves as a pre-chorus (Example 57). This phrase, like most of their songs, contains several melodic and lyrical hooks. At measure twenty, they introduce the first chromatic pitch, a B-flat in the key of the example. Its use is highlighted and made more special in the next measure, when they write a B-natural accompanying the word, "Stop." They repeat this great melodic and lyrical gesture in measures 22 and 23.

The entire eight-measure phrase serves as a pre-chorus and leads well into the repeat of the chorus.

Example 57: B-Phrase of Period II as Pre-Chorus

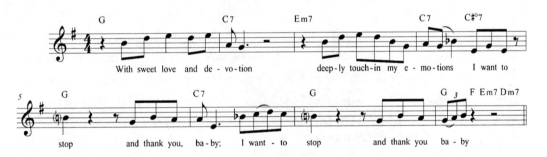

Verse/Chorus songs that include a pre-chorus might also include a bridge. The song, "Roar," (Example 58) made famous in a recording by the singer Katy Perry, does just that.

Example 58: Phrasal and Melodic Analysis of "Roar"

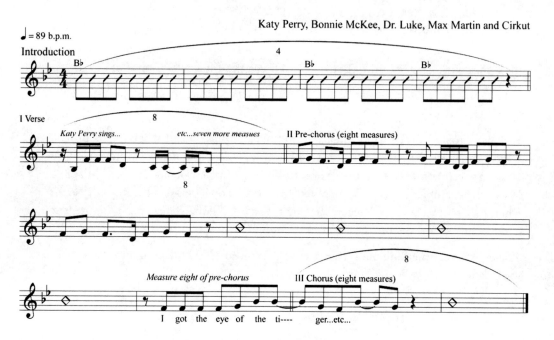

After a four-measure instrumental introduction, there is an eight-measure verse. An eight-measure pre-chorus follows the verse and leads directly to an eight-measure chorus. The chorus of this song is followed by a five-measure extension.

In the repeat, the verse is foreshortened to last just four measures. This is followed by a repeat of the eight-measure pre-chorus, an eight-measure chorus and then, an extension that is lengthened to a full eight measures.

At this point, the writers introduce a bridge of sorts. In the highly personal original recording, Ms. Perry repeats the title, "Roar" over a rhythmic ostinato for seven measures before repeating the chorus and its eight-measure extension.

Although a bit unconventional in its inclusion of the extensions after the choruses and the *sui generis* bridge, "Roar" does follow the general plan of the Verse/Chorus song with a pre-chorus. The melody of "Roar" is pentatonic. It uses the pitches in Example 59.

Example 59: Major Pentatonic Melody of "Roar"

The melody is composed exclusively of pitches from the pentatonic scale in B-flat

Many other Verse/Chorus songs add emphasis to the chorus by including an extension on some playings of the chorus. The extensions are usually only a few measures long, perhaps half the length of the entire chorus.

The song "Shake It Off" (Example 60) written by Bryan Michael Cox (1977-), Jermaine Dupri (1972-), Johntá Austin (1980-) and Carey (1969-) made famous in a recording by Mariah Carey, adds extensions to the chorus as does the song, "Jeremy" by Eddie Vedder (1964-) and Jeff Ament (1963-).

Example 60: "Shake It Off"

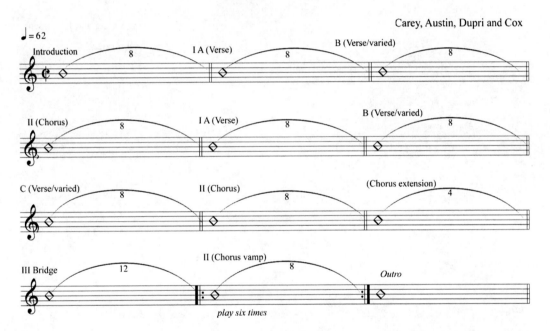

The writers of "Roar," like the writers of "Amazing Grace" and "How Sweet It Is," used only the pentatonic collection to create the melody.

Other Verse/Chorus songs that include a pre-chorus are: "You and I" (Ho, Stephens, Tozer and Wilson), "Don't Look Back in Anger" (by N. Gallagher) and "Royals" (by E. O'Connor and J. Little).

"Jeremy" was released in 1992 by the band, Pearl Jam. In "Jeremy," (Example 61) Vedder and Ament create a song that follows what is on the surface a simple Verse/Chorus form: There is an introduction of eight measures followed by a verse of eight measures.

Next, Vedder and Ament place a second verse that serves as a pre-chorus. It is a varied version of the verse that places Vedder's voice in a higher *tessitura*.

After the initial playing of the chorus, the verse and the varied verse/pre-chorus recurs to set up the second chorus. The chorus is then repeated and followed by a twelve-measure interlude that serves as a bridge. The interlude/bridge is followed by five playings of the eight-measure chorus period and a codetta or outro (a short phrase that ends the arrangement).

Example 61: "Jeremy"

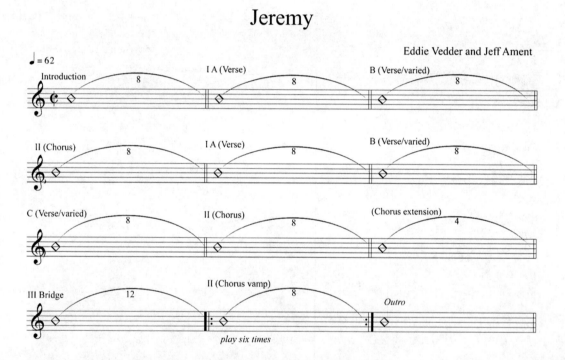

Many Verse/Chorus songs employ the solo-as-bridge strategy in recording. This is a perfect gambit to use in the production of a song that does not include a bridge. Sometimes, but not in this instance, the arranger creates a key change at the point when the chorus returns.

EXERCISES

Exercise #1

Analyze the melodic rhythm and lyrics of a verse/chorus song you like. Compose a new melody that uses the same melodic rhythm (and does not plagiarize the song you analyzed).

Exercise #2

Use the chord progression and harmonic rhythm below to compose the melody and lyrics for the Chorus Period of a new pop tune. The title of your song should be prominently featured in your lyrics. Base the title on a colloquial expression.

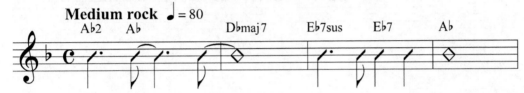

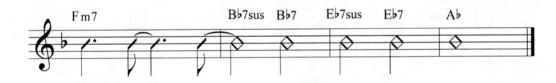

Exercise #3

Use the chord progression and harmonic rhythm below to compose the melody and lyrics for the Pre-Chorus of a new pop tune in Verse/Chorus Form.

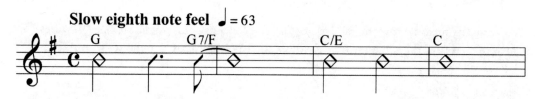

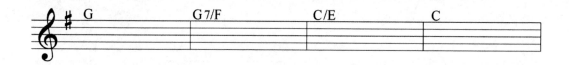

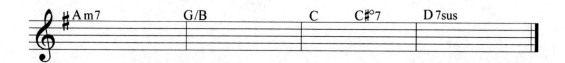

CHAPTER FOUR

TWENTIETH CENTURY BAR FORM

The second Double Period form we'll work with is what I call Twentieth Century Bar Form (TCBF). This is the form used in the writing of the majority of the songs found in the "Great American Songbook" – the name Tony Bennett invented for the canon of the most important, most influential and most recorded songs of the twentieth century. The Great American Songbook is principally made up of songs written for Broadway musical theatre and Hollywood musical films produced from the 1920s through the 1960s.

Songs in Twentieth Century Bar Form are characterized by their thirty-two measure length and the distinctive pattern of their phrases. Each period of a TCBF song is sixteen measures long and is composed of two eight-measure phrases.

Period one (labeled I in my examples) is composed of two eight-measure phrases, A^1 and A^2. Period two (labeled II) is composed of two eight-measure phrases labeled B and A^3.

The great success of the TCBF is based on the potency of its repeated A-phrase, the number of times the title hook is sung and the prominent placement of the title in the phrase. The A-phrase is sung three times with only minor musical variations. The variations are made to accommodate its repetition in Period I, the transition to the B-phrase in Period II and then to end the song as it is repeated after the B phrase.

The title is usually (but not always) repeated in each singing of the A-phrase. The placement of the title hook further undergirds the potency of the form since, since the title is sung in either the beginning or the end of each A-phrase.

HISTORY

Twentieth Century Bar Form is a variation of an older form simply called, *Bar Form*. The historic bar form is a two-section form whose parts follow a formal pattern of AAB.

During the Middle Ages, *Troubadours* created *ballades* in Bar Form. The troubadours were itinerant composers and performers who lived in Occitania, a region that roughly encompasses the southern half of France and parts of Italy and Spain. The troubadour tradition, life style and music influenced others to create similar movements and art. In northern France, the *trouvéres* and in Germany, the Minnesinger, like the troubadours, composed and performed songs whose lyrics dealt mainly with courtly love. The troubadour, trouvér and Minnesinger traditions declined during the fourteenth-century around the time of the Black Death, about 1348.

During the fourteenth-century in Germany, the Minnesingers' tradition gave way to the tradition of the *Meistersingers*. The Meistersingers were members of a guild for lyric poetry, composition and unaccompanied art song. The journeymen composers and poets of the Meistersinger guilds referred to their particularly artful works as *Bar*, most likely a shortening of *Barat*, a skillful thrusting move in fencing. The pattern of their songs was AAB: two repetitions of one melody (*Stollen*, meaning, stanzas) followed by a different melody (*Abgesang*, meaning *after song*). The Meistersingers used the term *Ton* (close enough to our modern, *tune*) to refer to one such complete song in Bar Form

The traditional Bar Form (AAB) can be found still in many Lutheran chorales (the hymn tunes that are sung by the congregation). As I have demonstrated in Chapter Two, American blues songs are also written with an AAB formal design.

ANOTHER ANTECEDENT

Stephen Collins Foster (1826-1864), known to some as the "father of American Popular music," was the country's first successful composer of popular songs. Foster wrote the music and lyrics for more than two hundred songs, and enjoyed great success during his lifetime. Foster's songs were regularly performed in recital, in homes and were arranged for the popular brass and percussion bands of the day. Several of Foster's songs are still popular, and often heard. These include "Oh! Susanna," "Camptown Races," "Old Folks at Home," "My Old Kentucky Home," "Jeanie with the Light Brown Hair," "Old Black Joe," and "Beautiful Dreamer."

Both "Beautiful Dreamer" and "Jeanie with the Light Brown Hair" were written using short phrases. "Beautiful Dreamer" is in a sectional ABA form; "Jeanie with the Light Brown Hair" is in AABA form. The opening phrase of "Beautiful Dreamer" is eight measures long. It's harmonic progression is circular: it starts and ends on the tonic. This is followed by a B-phrase that is just four measures long. The B-phrase is also circular: it begins and ends on the dominant. Foster returns to the opening melody for a truncated version of the A-phrase. (It is just six measures long.)

Stephen Foster's "Jeannie with the Light Brown Hair" (Example 62) is composed in a small AABA form. The beginning A-phrases are each just four measures. Foster varies the second A to provide a melodic high point at its end. The B-phrase is contrasting in its melodic rhythm, lyrics and purpose—it is a circular phrase that begins on the dominant harmony and also ends there. Foster repeats the A-phrase at the end of the song. He varies it again, this time to have it end on a final tonic harmony.

I consider both songs as forerunners of the Twentieth Century Bar Form that I will discuss next.

Example 62: Leadsheet Analysis of "Jeannie with the Light Brown Hair"

Jeannie with the Light Brown Hair

Stephen Foster

While Stephen Foster's song is half the length of typical Twenty-first Century songs in the AABA form, it nevertheless shows the same essential pattern of phrase construction.

TWENTIETH CENTURY BAR FORM AND ROUNDED BINARY

In the early part of the twentieth century, American and British songwriters working in popular music began to modify the traditional bar form pattern (AAB) in couple of ways, most importantly by adding a repeat of the A-phrase in the second period (after the B-phrase). These modifications yielded the two-period song of the TCBF with phrases presented as AABA. Other modifications and variations were made, too. We will look at these a little later in this chapter.

Twentieth Century Bar Form closely resembles the formal design of much longer compositions that are said to be in *Rounded Binary Form*. Rounded Binary Form consists of two periods, thus the binary designation, where the first period recurs after the playing of the second period. The B-phrase of pop tunes in Twentieth Century Bar Form, like second-periods in Rounded Binary Form, are usually in a key different from that of the A-period.

An Enduring Form

The Twentieth Century Bar Form became the most common form during the first half of the twentieth century. The popular songs from this period in American music history are also called *standards* since their popularity has endured and so many performers have so often recorded them.

The Twentieth Century Bar Form remains a touchstone amongst professional songwriters. Best-selling songwriters as individual in their styles as Billy Joel ("New York State of Mind"), James Taylor ("Don't Let Me Be Lonely Tonight"), Thelonious Monk ("Round Midnight"), Carole King and Gerry Goffin ("Will You Still Love Me Tomorrow"), John Lennon and Paul McCartney ("Yesterday"), Richard Rogers and Lorenz Hart ("My Funny Valentine"), and Billie Joe Armstrong ("Wake Me Up When September Ends"), have all written successfully in Twentieth Century Bar Form.

In the next sections, I present in detail the characteristics that make this form special.

The Harmonic Motion of the Periods

The two periods of a Twentieth Century Bar Form song are balanced: they are each eight measures long. The A-phrases of a Twentieth Century Bar Form song are called *verses*, while the B-phrase is called the *bridge*.

The verse of a Twentieth Century Bar Form song is presented twice at the beginning of the song. To facilitate the repeat of the verse, the composer will end the first verse on a dominant. To make the transition to the bridge, the composer sounds a dominant of the key of the bridge. Bridges of songs in Twentieth Century Bar Form are usually composed in a new contrasting, but complimentary, key. The bridge ends in such a way as to facilitate an easy transition back to the key of the verse.

THE TITLE IS THE HOOK

Unlike verses in Verse/Chorus songs, verses in Twentieth Century Bar Form songs always contain the song's lyrical and melodic hook. The lyrical hook of the Twentieth Century Bar Form song is always the song's title.

The title hook is most often placed at one of two places: Either at the beginning of the verse or at the end of the verse. Listen through the Twentieth Century Bar Form songs I have listed at the beginning of this chapter. You will find that in the songs, "New York State of Mind," "Don't Let Me Be Lonely," "Will You Still Love Me Tomorrow," and "Wake Me Up When September Ends," the composer places the title hook at the end of the verses. The composers of "Yesterday" and "My Funny Valentine," placed the title hook at the beginning of the verse. A complete sampling of Twentieth Century Bar Form songs would probably show a fairly equal distribution of title hook placements.

A BRIDGE PROVIDES CONTRAST

The bridges of all Twentieth Century Bar Form songs provide contrast in one of two ways: Bridges are usually in a new key (or will hint at one); their melodic rhythm will usually be different from that of the verse. If the verse features a melody made up of quick notes, the melody of the bridge might have a slower pace.

ANALYSIS OF "WAKE ME UP WHEN SEPTEMBER ENDS"

A closer look at the song, "Wake Me Up When September Ends" (Example 63) will demonstrate how contemporary composers make use of the venerable Twentieth Century Bar Form.

Released in 2005 on the band, Green Day's album, American Idiot, "Wake Me Up When September Ends," is a perfect example of the TCBF form. The song, written by lead singer, Billie Joe Armstrong and the band, is in thirty-two measures and strictly follows the AABA phrase structure of the Twentieth Century Bar Form.

Example 63: "Wake Me Up When September Ends"

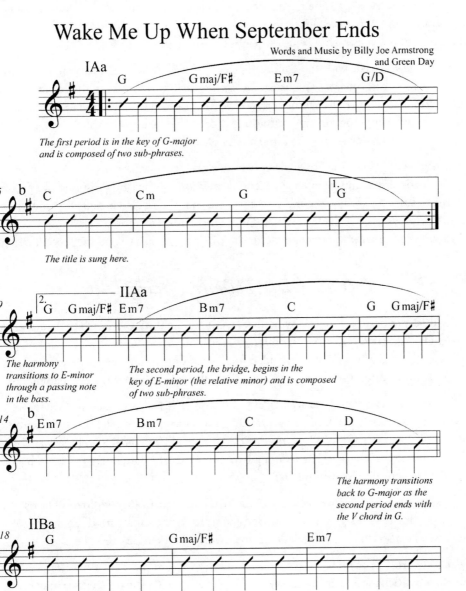

Wake Me Up When September Ends

Words and Music by Billy Joe Armstrong
and Green Day

*The first period is in the key of G-major
and is composed of two sub-phrases.*

The title is sung here.

*The harmony
transitions to E-minor
through a passing note
in the bass.*

*The second period, the bridge, begins in the
key of E-minor (the relative minor) and is composed
of two sub-phrases.*

*The harmony transitions
back to G-major as the
second period ends with
the V chord in G.*

*The second period concludes
with a restatement of the opening
A-phrase.*

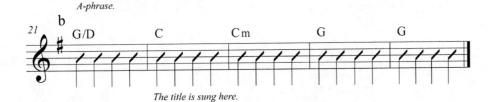

The title is sung here.

The song begins with an eight-measure A-phrase that is immediately repeated to form the first period of the song. The creators of the song place its title-hook at the end of each iteration of the A-phrases. The second period, like all second periods in TCBF songs, begins with the B-phrase, a bridge of eight measures.

The bridge contrasts with the A-phrase verses. The A-phrases of the original recording are in the key of G-major. The bridge begins in the key of E-minor, the relative minor of G-major. The term relative minor or relative major is used to describe the relationship between two keys, one major, one minor, whose tonic lie a minor third (or major sixth) apart where each key shares the same pitch collection.

The bridge of "Wake Me" only visits E-minor briefly: It transitions back to the home key of G-major almost immediately, in the third measure of the bridge, during the first four-measure sub-phrase. The second four-measure sub-phrase also begins in E-minor and transitions back to G-major in its third measure. The entire bridge ends on the dominant harmony of G-major to facilitate the repeat of the A-phrase to end the second period.

SOME ADDITIONAL FEATURES

In addition to very strictly following the Twentieth-Century Bar Form in their use of precisely thirty-two measures, the phrase pattern of AABA and the placement of the hook at the end of the A-phrases, Billie Joe Armstrong and his band mates employed two other features often found in pop songs. First, they make use of the descending bass line.

The use of a bass line that descends, either diatonically (as is the case in "Wake Me Up When September Ends"), of chromatically (as in our next example) is so often employed in popular music that it can be considered idiomatic. (The British composer, Henry Purcell employed this bassline technique in, "When I Am Laid in Earth" from his opera *Dido and Aeneas* from around 1688.)

The second quite common technique employed by Armstrong and Green Day is to move the harmony from IV (the major subdominant) to iv, the minor subdominant. As I have discussed earlier, this is an example of borrowing or modal mixture.

The standard, "My Funny Valentine" (Example 64) from the 1937 Broadway show, *Babes in Arms* by Richard Rodgers and Lorenz Hart is also in Twentieth Century Bar Form.

Like "Wake Me When September Ends," it features a descending bass line, only this time the bass line is chromatic, and has a bridge that moves to the relative key.

Example 64: Harmonic Motion of "My Funny Valentine"

My Funny Valentine

Music by Richard Rodgers
Lyrics by Lorenz Hart

"My Funny Valentine" begins in our example in the key of C-minor. The first period is composed of two eight-measure phrases. The first phrase ends on the dominant of C-minor, facilitating the repeat. The second A-phrase ends on the dominant of the key of the bridge, E-flat major. E-flat major is the relative major of C-minor. As we saw in "Wake Me When September Ends," moving harmonically from a minor key to its relative major or vice versa provides harmonic contrast and a degree of novelty that keeps the listener interested in hearing more of the song. Most listeners will not identify this kind of harmonic change in the same way as will a trained musician, but most do sense that something novel has happened.

When the composer Rodgers returns us to the home key of C-minor, I believe that most listeners feel a sense of comfort at having arrived back to where the song began. The sense of departure, of movement away from the original harmony, and then returning home is a significant feature of the Twentieth Century Bar Form and often exploited too well by songwriters. Not all TCBF songs move to the relative major or minor key.

A song I wrote called "Gentle Heart" (Example 65) is published in a choral arrangement. The verses of this song are composed in the key of A-major. The bridge moves, suddenly, to C-major. Although they have some pitches in common (A, B, D and E), A-major and C-major are not closely related. This is what theorists consider a *remote key relationship*.

Example 65: Moving To Key Other Than Relative Minor for the Bridge

I move from the key of the verses to the key of the bridge with no preparation at all, except that in measure eight, the dominant chord, E[7], is preceded by the dominant of C-major: the G chord. The G chord sounded in the key of A-major is quite striking because its root is the flat-seven of A-major. I will argue that the G chord does resonate with listeners and does, in fact, foreshadow the harmonic move I make to defeat A-major and supplant it with the key of C-major.

The transition back to the key of A-major is convincing and complete as I move in measure seven of the bridge to a minor subdominant (iv) and then the dominant of A-major. The minor version of A's subdominant is borrowed from the key of A-minor, where one finds a D_m chord build on the subdominant. I then move (in measure eight) to the dominant of both A-major and A-minor, E^7. Once there, I can easily move the song back to the home key of A-major.

Lyrical Characteristics of Twentieth Century Bar Form

The lyric is unique for each iteration for the verse in a Twentieth Century Bar Form song. Verses are strophic, except that the title hook is usually repeated at the same spot with each new line of lyrics.

I have shown, though, in the Rodgers and Hart example, "My Funny Valentine," that lyricists do not always strictly follow the rules. Another notable illustration of not following the rules is a song we have discussed before, "Yesterday," by Lennon and McCartney.

The title, "Yesterday" appears at the very start of the song. Just like in "My Funny Valentine," it is the first word of the verse sung over a very powerful but simple melodic motive. The word, "yesterday" is also the last word of the first verse.

In the second verse, the melodic motive is again heard in the first measure, but this time it is accompanied by the word, "suddenly." The word, "suddenly" also appears at the end of the second verse. Its appearance at the end is made more poignant as Lennon and McCartney make it part of a line using the word, "yesterday."

> "Oh, yesterday came suddenly."

The third verse also begins and ends with the title hook, "Yesterday." The third verse appears, of course, after the bridge. The bridge for "Yesterday" moves harmonically to the relative minor of the home key (The song is in F-major; the bridge moves to D-minor.)

One might conclude that, while it's a fine idea to learn the rules, judging by the success of "Yesterday" and "My Funny Valentine," it's also a fine idea to break the rules you learn.

VARIATIONS

THE INTRODUCTORY VERSE

Many songs for Broadway shows or movie musicals from the 1920s through the 1950s
written in Twentieth Century Bar Form include an *introductory verse*. An introductory
verse is a rambling sixteen- to thirty-two measure period whose lyric provides a context
for the song that is to follow: It sets the stage for the singer to unfold the story of the
song proper. The introductory verse for "My Funny Valentine" (Example 66) is typical of
the periods used to begin many Twentieth Century Bar Form songs.

Example 66: Introductory Verse of "My Funny Valentine"

Codetta

A *codetta* is a brief section of music that is added to the main portion of a song to announce the song's conclusion. The songs used in this chapter's examples include a codetta in their original form. Here are the codettas for "Yesterday" (Example 67) and "My Funny Valentine" (Example 68).

Example 67: Codetta of "Yesterday"

The codetta ends with the opening rhythmic motive adding continuity to the song.

Example 68: Codetta of "My Funny Valentine"

The codetta allows the composer to conclude the song in the relative major key

Other Songs in Twentieth Century Bar Form

Other songs in Twentieth Century Bar Form include:
- "At Last" (Harry Warren and Mack Gordon)
- "Blue Moon" (Richard Rodgers and Lorenz Hart)
- "Bye Bye Blackbird" (Mort Dixon and Ray Henderson)
- "Five Feet Two, Eyes of Blue" (Sam Lewis, Joe Young and Ray Henderson)
- "I Get a Kick Out of You" (Cole Porter)
- "I Got Rhythm" (George and Ira Gershwin)
- "Jingle-Bell Rock" (Joe Beal and Jim Boothe)
- "The Lady is a Tramp" (Lorenz Hart and Richard Hart)

For your convenience, a template of the Twentieth Century Bar Form is included. On the template, you will find the periods, phrases, and sub-phrases indicated along with the possible locations of the title hook.

Example 69: Twentieth Century Bar Form Template

Exercises

In my personal experience coaching aspiring songwriters, I have found that most students have difficulties writing songs in Twentieth Century Bar Form. I suppose this might be because the form is no longer as popular as it once was and is therefore "not in their ears." Most often, student songwriters instead compose a Verse/Chorus song.

Some careful listening to older songs from the standard pop repertoire usually cures this problem. To that end, I have supplied above a short list of pop songs in this now elusive, but worth learning, form.

Exercise #1

Compose one eight-measure period that can end with either a tonic or a dominant. (It is acceptable to resolve on a tonic and then move to a ii—V cadence.)

Exercise #2

Develop a concise phrase that will become a title hook. Use any of the songs in the supplied list as a model.

Compose only the melodic hook that will accompany this title hook. Compose it in 3/4 meter in a key you are not totally used to working in. (Guitar players might want to choose a flat key.)

Exercise #3

Compose a hit song in Twentieth Century Bar Form using the template in Example 69, whose lyrics sing about something other than romantic love. At this point, this should be a simple assignment.

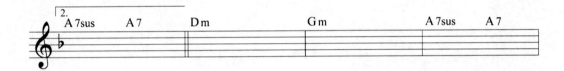

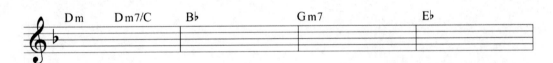

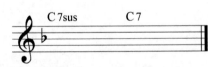

This exercise features both the I-vi-ii-V and the iii-IV-ii-V progressions. Use it to create the first period of a Twentieth Century Bar Form song. Note the second ending. It transitions the piece to D-minor for the bridge of the song. Optional: Complete the song's final eight measures using the material from the first period. Feel free to compose a codetta, too.

CHAPTER FIVE

POP SONG BINARY FORM

Like almost all Twentieth Century Bar Form songs, songs in *Pop Song Binary Form* (Pop Binary Form), are usually thirty-two measures long. The thirty-two measures of the Binary Form Pop Songs are divided into two distinct sixteen-measure periods, labeled I and II in my examples. Each sixteen-measure period consists of two balanced eight measure phrases, labeled A, B and C. The periods and phrases are ordered as shown in Example 70.

Each eight-measure phrase, A, B and C, are commonly divided into two four-measure sub-phrases. In Pop Song Binary Form, the A-phrase repeats at the beginning of the second period. This kind of construction is called, *parallel construction* . Parallel construction yields a phrase structure that lays out as A B A C, where A and B form the first period (I) and A and C form the second period (II).

Example 70: Pop Song Binary Form Template

Pop Song Binary Form Template

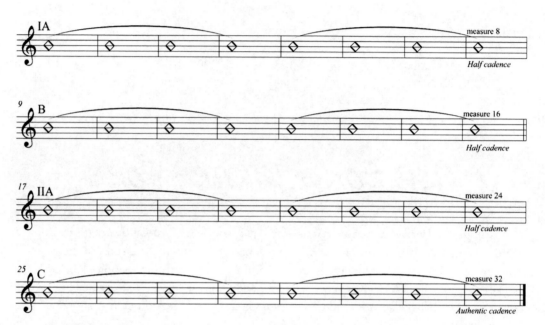

There are four small periods, each eight measures long. They are A, B and C. The small A period
is repeated beginning at measure 17.

There are two large periods, each is sixteen measures long. They are marked I and II.
Each consists of two smaller (eight measure) periods. Large Period I is measures 1 through 16;
Large Period II is measures 17 through 32.

Harmonic Motion and Cadences

The Pop Song Binary Form is all about delaying resolution. The main goal of the
composer writing in this form is to avoid a final sounding authentic cadence. An
authentic cadence is a harmonic progression moving from the dominant to the tonic. In
well-written pop binary songs, the authentic cadence is delayed until the very end of the
song.

DELAYED LYRICAL CONCLUSION

In every Pop Binary Form song there are a few concluding words in the last line that sum up the song's sentiment. This lyrical punch line also includes a restatement of the song's title. Let's look at some examples of lyrics for songs in this venerable form. We will begin with "The Days of Wine and Roses," (Example 71) a song written by lyricist Johnny Mercer and composer Henry Mancini.

Example 71: Lyrics "The Days of Wine and Roses"

The Days of Wine and Roses (by lyricist Johnny Mercer and composer Henry Mancini)

I A

> The Days of Wine and Roses
> laugh and run away,
> like a child at play

B

> Through a meadowland toward a closing door,
> A door marked, "never more,"
> That wasn't there before.

IIA

> The lonely night discloses
> Just a passing breeze,
> filled with memories

*Johnny Mercer
(1909-1976)*

C

> Of the golden smile that introduced me to,
> The Days of Wine and Roses...
> And you.

A beautiful love affair has ended. All that is left are the wonderful memories of the "golden smile" that caught the spokesperson's eye and began this romance with libation and flowers. The very object of this person's affection, the lover whose smile is golden, is not mentioned until the penultimate line of the lyric. Then, in the kicker, the punch line at the end of this very poetic lyric, is the inclusion of the words, "and you."

By making this song's lyric non-specific, Mercer makes it universal. He could have named names ("The wine I shared with Shirley"?), but he wisely chose not to. Instead, Mercer created a lyric that most adults can understand at a visceral level.

Let us analyze another. "Here's That Rainy Day" (Example 72) is a song written by composer Jimmy Van Heusen and lyricist Johnny Burke for the 1953 Broadway show, *Carnival in Flanders.*

This Pop Binary song, like many in this form, is very popular amongst thoughtful creative musicians. We will look at the lyrics for this song and come back to the music for this one and the Mancini tune later.

Example 72: Lyrics "Here's That Rainy Day"

Here's That Rainy Day (Lyrics by Johnny Burke)

IA

Maybe I should have saved those leftover dreams,
Funny, but Here's That Rainy Day.

B

Here's that rainy day they told me about,
And I laughed at the thought that it might turn our this way.

IIA

Where is that worn out wish that I threw aside,
After it brought my lover near?

C

Funny, how love becomes a cold, rainy day.
Funny that rainy day is here.

In "Here's That Rainy Day" Johnny Burke weaves another recollection of love gone sour. Using the metaphor of a rainy day to represent love's loss, Burke paints a sad tale that matches well Van Heusen's poignant melody and harmony. This is what the spokesperson was warned about, and he dismissed: If one loves, one can be hurt. Chagrined, the spokesperson admits in the final line of the lyric that, indeed, that "rainy day is here." This is the not-so-funny punch line, the kicker, of this great standard.

Not all Pop Binary Form songs have sad lyrics. The song, "My Romance" mentioned earlier, is from the Broadway musical and film, *Jumbo,* by composer Richard Rodgers and lyricist Lorenz Hart. It sings about love gone right! The lyrics for this song are what the songwriter, Bill Pere, calls a *list song.*

In "My Romance" (Example 73), Hart beautifully enumerates all the many things that his romance does not need. Then, at the kicker in the last line of the lyric, Hart writes that his romance "doesn't need a thing but you." The writers create so many beautiful images in this lyric and then dismiss out of hand as being unnecessary to achieve romantic fulfillment. Thankfully, the only component the spokesperson truly needs is the lover.

Many pop binary songs mention the title hook very few times. This is not the case with "My Romance." The title hook appears in every phrase of the song.

Example 73: Lyrics "My Romance"

My Romance (Lyrics by Lorenz Hart)

IA

My Romance doesn't have to have a moon in the sky
My romance doesn't need a blue lagoon standing by

B

No month of May, no twinkling stars.
No hideaway, no soft guitars.

IIA

My Romance doesn't need a castle rising in Spain
Nor a dance to a constantly surprising refrain

C

Wide awake, I can make my most fantastic dreams come true.
My Romance doesn't need a thing but you!

HARMONIC AND MELODIC ANALYSIS OF "THE DAYS OF WINE AND ROSES"

In "The Days of Wine and Roses" (Example 74), Mancini begins each phrase with a pick-up note or two. This gives the song with a sense of moving forward and provides a balance for the many long notes of the great melody. Each eight-measure phrase is divided into two four-measure sub-phrase (note that I have indicated that the phrases begin with the pick-up notes).

Mancini's harmony is chock-full of modal mixture (combining in one phrase the harmonies common in more than one mode) and allusions to other key centers. For instance, in measure two he writes an Eb9. This is an extremely provocative chord to introduce in the very beginning of a song! It does not occur in the key of F-major, the indicated tonal center of the piece. "Where is he going, harmonically?" is what a listener's subconscious might ask. The Eb9 proceeds immediately to a D7 chord, causing me to realize that Mancini was thinking of the Eb9 as a *tritone substitution* for D's normal dominant. (Or, my classical theory geek's mind reminds that I could hear this dominant ninth chord as a kind of enharmonically spelled German augmented sixth chord, of course.) Either way, Mancini moves to the dominant of ii, which was his harmonic target all along.

What Mancini has done so successfully in these five measures is create a new version of an old progression found in several songs, including for instance, "Georgia On My Mind" by composer Hoagy Carmichael (1899-1981) and lyricist Stuart Gorrell (1901-1963). Thinking in the same key as is Mancini's song, "Georgia" would begin on the tonic, F, and then move harmonically to the dominant (A7) of vi, (Dm). Mancini follows essentially the same harmonic progression, but uses the *tritone substitute* to lead to D7.

Mancini uses a half cadence to end each phrase, as is common in pop binary songs. However, at the end of the A-phrases, he wrote a half cadence in Ab major, not F major. Then, instead of resolving on Ab, he resolves to Am, the harmony a tritone away.

The *tritone* abounds in "Wine and Roses." In measures two and eight, and again in measures eighteen and twenty-four, the melody note, A, is written. This pitch is an augmented fourth above the chord root, Eband demonstrates Mancini's further use of modal mixture, this time borrowing from the Lydian mode.

Like all Pop Binary songs, Mancini creates a climax in the melody near the end of the song. In "The Days of Wine and Roses" the melodic climax occurs at measures twenty-seven and twenty-eight on the word, "to." The melody note, E, is the leading tone in this key and is the highest note of the song. Mancini follows the climax with a gentle winding down of the melody over the next two measures. He gently lands the melody on the tonic to accompany the final word of the song, "you."

Example 74: "The Days of Wine and Roses"

"The Days of Wine and Roses"

Music by Henry Mancini
Lyrics by Johnny Mercer

Like all double binary songs, "The Days of Wine and Roses" is composed of a total of thirty-two measures, arranged in four eight-measure periods. There are half cadences at the end of each eight-measure period, except for the final period (C). It ends with an authentic cadence in the home key.

OTHER SONGS IN POP BINARY SONG FORM

Other songs in Pop Binary Song Form include:
- "A Day in the Life of a Fool" (Carl Sigman and Luiz Bonfa)
- "All of Me" (Seymour Simons and Gerald Marks)
- "Bill Bailey Won't You Please Come Home?" (Hughie Cannon)
- "But Not For Me" (George and Ira Gershwin)
- "I Thought About You" (Jimmy Van Heusen and Johnny Mercer)
- "Emily" (Johnny Mandel and Johnny Mercer)
- "Someday My Prince Will Come" (Frank Churchill and Larry Morey)
- "There Will Never Be Another You" (Harry Warren and Mack Gordon)
- "Yesterdays" (Jerome Kern and Otto Harbach)
- "I'll See You in My Dreams" (Gus Kahn and Isham Jones)
- "Laura" (Johnny Mercer and David Raskin)
- "Lullaby of Broadway" (Al Dubin and Harry Warren)

Exercises

There is only one assignment for this chapter.
Use the template below to create several songs in the Pop Song Binary Form.

Period I

A (sub-phrase a)
antecedent phrase

Key One

A (sub-phrase b)
consequent phrase

5

Some kind of incomplete authentic cadence; a half-cadence or dominant of the next new key.

B (sub-phrase a)
antecedent phrase

9

Possible temporary move to new key center.

B (sub-phrase b)
consequent phrase

13

Half-cadence allowing for repetition of opening material.

Period II

A (sub-phrase a)
antecedent phrase

17

Key One
(measures 17 through 24 are essentially the same material as measures 1 through 8)

A (sub-phrase b)
consequent phrase

21

Some kind of incomplete authentic cadence; a half-cadence or dominant of the next new key.

C (sub-phrase a)
antecedent phrase

25

(Measures 24 through 32 contain new material, perhaps based on the B phrase of Period I, providing a resolution to the musical tension created in previous sections. In this phrase, the lyrics are also summed up.)

C (sub-phrase b)
consequent phrase

29

Complete authentic cadence providing close for the song.

CHAPTER SIX

LYRICS

A song's lyrics provide the listener with a direct connection to the writer's heart (or at least her mind). But, good lyrics do not only speak to the listener, they speak on behalf of the listener and provide an opportunity for the listener to identify with the singer. In song, the singer becomes a kind of Everyman who puts into song the things we all sometimes feel but very often cannot quite find the right words to express. Listeners hear the meaning of the words, but are also emotionally moved by the music.

THE MOST IMPORTANT LINK TO THE LISTENER

Melody, harmony and rhythm communicate to listeners on a more basic level than do the lyrics. Humans give meaning to music because of many things, including learned interpretations, social context, habit and, according to researcher Elizabeth Tolbert of the Peabody Conservatory, "conditions that are biologically grounded in our evolutionary history." Musical meaning is sensed on a primal level, as is touch and smell. Sound, in this case melody and accompaniment, quite literally moves the listener. But no matter how catchy or memorable, music remains abstract in its meaning. A song's lyrics supply the part most listeners understand immediately and remember most. The rest they "get" on some kind of subconscious level.

ONE BIG THOUGHT SAID IN PLAIN ENGLISH

Lyrics are best when they are written in vernacular English. Everyday language that is easily understood by the majority of listeners will provide the most direct path to understanding the songwriter's message.

Songs can be about most anything, but must always express just one emotion — happiness, sadness, love, hate, fear, hope, agitation or sorrow. Even songs with lots of patter (the term music people use to describe wordy, rapid-fire lyrics) must contain just one message.

Billy Joel's song, "We Didn't Start the Fire," is very wordy! Here's the opening:

Example 75: Lyrics to "We Didn't Start the Fire"

"We Didn't Start the Fire" written by Billy Joel

VERSE:

> Harry Truman, Doris Day, Red China, Johnnie Ray,
> South Pacific, Walter Winchell, Joe DiMaggio,
> Joe McCarthy, Richard Nixon, Studebaker, television
> North Korea, South Korea, Marilyn Monroe,
> Rosenbergs, H-bomb, Sugar Ray, Panmunjom
> Brando, "The King and I" and "The Catcher in the Rye"
> Eisenhower, vaccine, England's got a new queen,
> Marciano, Liberace, Santayana goodbye

The message is simple, though: The world is a mess—we did not make it this way!

CHORUS:

> We didn't start the fire
> It was always burning
> Since the world's been turning
> We didn't start the fire
> No we didn't light it
> But we tried to fight it

Notice a few things about this infinitely clever lyric:

Joel creates a sense of controlled confusion with his list of names and things sung in patter. From the start, we have no real clear idea what is happening. The words are familiar, but why they are juxtaposed as they are? We do not know, and we will not know until the singer gets us to the chorus.

The confusion is made appealing for a few reasons. First, the words chosen are titillating and their juxtaposition, provocative. Next, Joel seasons the list with an occasional internal rhyme: *(Doris) Day, (Johnny) Ray; (North) Korea, (South) Korea; "(King and) I" and "(Catcher in the) Rye," vaccine and queen.* Rhymes help anchor a lyric and, along with the melodic rhythm, help the listener hear and remember what is being sung.

The meaning of the words of the verse is made clearer once the title is sung in the chorus: "We Didn't Start the Fire." Somehow, all these other folks and things started the metaphorical fire, not us. The present-day mess is just what always is, but we didn't make it so. The other lyrics of the chorus support the proposition put forth in the title: This mess has always been with us and, try as we might to alter the condition of the human experience; it is still pretty much a mess.

LYRICS ARE POETIC, BUT NOT POEMS

The lyric to Billy Joel's "We Didn't Start the Fire" is much denser than are the lyrics to most popular songs. Lyrics are generally more like the sentiments on a greeting card than they are like a scholarly poem. Pop song lyrics need to be easily grasped and remembered because music is ephemeral: It occurs in the performance and then vanishes into the ether. Poems, even those that are read aloud, are read, pondered for their meaning and sometimes read again. A reader can return to a line or a stanza without much difficulty; song lyrics are "once and done" until the next time the song is played.

LYRICS, A COMPOSITE OF THE WRITER'S EXPERIENCE

From time to time, we all are moved to express a feeling, describe an event or memorialize a person. I often find in writing lyrics that new song lyrics often are a conflation of ideas and experiences from various times in my life, reading I have done, movies and television shows I have viewed and other songs that I have heard.

Songwriting can be inspired, but inspiration is not a mystical occurrence. Inspiration is the result of the desire to express something in a novel way, experience and much effort. The lyricist Sammy Cahn was once asked, "what comes first: the music or the lyrics?" The master wordsmith quickly replied, "Neither. The phone call comes first." In other words, Cahn was saying, give me a reason to write and an idea about what it is that is needed for the project and I will put sincere and extreme effort into crafting a novel way to write about a subject drawn from my experiences and expertise.

THE SUBJECT OF YOUR SONG

Songs can be about most anything. The subject matter for a song can evolve from anywhere. Characters and plot lines can be drawn from life experiences including people watching, reading or classic scenarios recast in your personal voice.

Whatever the subject matter, lyrics always express one clear message that is usually summed up in the song's title. The title and the singular message of the song is supported and amplified in the remainder of the song's lyrics. Any line or word that does not substantively further the essential message of the title does not belong in the song and must be edited out.

Where do ideas come from? Everywhere and anywhere: newspapers, blogs, magazines, television, conversations overheard and...other songs.

SOMETHING TO WRITE ABOUT

When no one is calling to commission a song, you can create your own commission by establishing parameters of a proposed song. Defining what you propose to write might go something like this: "I want to write a song that has the same kind of gist as some other song." Or, "I want to write a song in g-minor that has the feel of an updated version of James Brown's, "On the Good Foot."

By defining the parameters of your proposed song, you will avoid the most frightening aspect of a professional life in a creative occupation: the blank page.

Many writers, composers and songwriters included, become paralyzed when offered the opportunity to write *anything*. The paralysis is made worse only when one is working on a commission and the client says, "Oh, you know what to do. Just write anything." Rest assured–there is a great possibility that whatever you write will be wrong!

By creating a set of rules for what your proposed song is not going to be, you are clearly defining what it will be. Other things you might want to define at the beginning of the creative songwriting process include what kind of singer you are writing for, who your audience might be, what genre you are writing in, what the tempo will be, what the instrumentation might be and so on. By placing limits on our creative selves, we actually speed along a writing process that might otherwise languish.

Let's look at a song I co-wrote with Philip Hardin as a case study.

Phil came to my studio one afternoon in February or March with some good ideas for a Christmas cha-cha that was also a love song.

I thought these were outstanding concepts and quickly suggested we might model the song's lyric after the story related in the Christmas pop classic, "I Saw Mommy Kissing Santa Clause." I also suggested we write in a major key and in a Twentieth Century Bar Form (AABA).

We had it all: The form, the feel, the tempo, the lyrical concept and the kind of singer (it had to be a woman with a cute, but solid pop-mezzo). All we needed now was thirty-two measures of hit melody and accompaniment and a bunch of words that said the same kind of things as "I Saw Mommy Kissing Santa Clause," but in a unique un-plagiarizing way! In a little more than an hour, Phil and I had created the song "Nick and Me" (Example 76).

All we needed now was thirty-two measures of hit melody and accompaniment and a bunch of words that said the same kind of things as "I Saw Mommy Kissing Santa Clause,"...

Example 76: Leadsheet for "Nick & Me"

Nick and Me
A Christmas Cha Cha

Music by Louis deLise
Lyrics by Louis deLise and Phil Hardin

In no way does "Nick & Me" resemble its model, except that the narrator expresses affection for this person pretending to be St. Nicholas.

Such modeling is not the exception. It is the usual. As the Italian scholar, Umberto Eco wrote:

> "Until then I had thought each book spoke of things, human or divine, that lie outside books. Now I realize that not infrequently books speak of books; it is as if they spoke among themselves."

Songs speak to other songs; songwriters often model their new creations on those of other songwriters.

THE PROSODY OF THE LYRICS MUST MATCH THE RHYTHM OF THE MELODY

All melodies have a rhythm and the lyricist must conform to that rhythm by matching the accents of the lyrics to the accents in the melody. The term, *prosody* is used to mean the rhythm of language. The accents of the melody (that are reinforced by the accents of the undergirding accompaniment), must directly coincide with the accents of the lyrics otherwise the words will be misheard and misunderstood by the listener. The listener's ability to understand a word is lessened when that word is pronounced with incorrect prosody: with the syllables incorrectly accented.

CORRECT PROSODY

The word, *romance*, can be pronounced with the strong accent occurring on either the first or second syllable: either, ro´-mance or ro-mance´.

Ah, what to do? Here is how two different songwriting teams answered the question.

In the great standard of 1936, "A Fine Romance" (Example 77) by composer Jerome Kern and lyricist, Dorothy Fields, the word is accented on the first syllable:

Example 77: Opening line of "A Fine Romance"

In the song "My Romance" (Example 78) written for the 1935 Broadway show, *Jumbo*, by Lorenz Hart and Richard Rodgers the word is accented on the second syllable:

Example 78: Opening line of "My Romance"

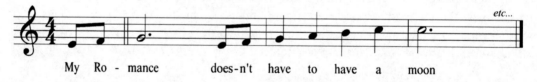

In both songs, the lyricist handles the issue of the lyrical prosody by placing the accented syllable on the *downbeat* of the measure. The downbeat is the name given to the first beat of a measure. It is so-called because this is the direction and placement of a conductor's hand on this beat. Musicians performing Western pop music always give the strongest accent to the first beat of the measure.

THE TITLE IS THE PRIMARY LYRICAL HOOK

All great song lyrics, like "We Didn't Start the Fire," "My Romance" and "A Fine Romance" will have many hooks, but the most important lyrical hook is always the song's title.

CHARACTERISTICS

The song's title will always be accompanied by the most important musical hook or motive and, because this is the most important thing for a listener to remember, lyricists will always place the title in a significant and easy to remember spot in the song.

PLACEMENT OF THE TITLE

Songwriters want people to remember the title so that they can buy the song.

Table 7: Title Placement Based on Form

Form	Title Placement
Single Period Form (AAA)	The title will be placed at the start of the first phrase
Verse/Chorus Form (ABAB)	The title will be placed at the beginning or the end of the chorus, or in both places. The lyricist may also choose to place the title at the end of the verse or pre-chorus, just before the chorus.
Twentieth Century Bar Form (AABA)	The title will be placed at the beginning or the end of the A sections and almost never in the bridge (the B section).
Pop Song Binary Form	The title will be placed at the start of the first period, and often at the start of the second period and at the conclusion of the song.

RHYMING AND OTHER POETIC DEVICES USED IN LYRICS

Like most poetry, songwriters often include rhyming words in their lyrics. When words rhyme, listeners notice them. Rhymes echo in the listener's mind, help emphasize certain points and make the language of the song memorable.

Two words or the end syllables of two words are said to rhyme if they sound exactly alike, except for their initial consonant sound. When lyricists place rhymes at the end of a line of text, this is called an *end rhyme* or *terminal rhyme*. When a lyricist rhymes a word in the middle of a line of text with the last word of a line or if two words in the middle of a line rhyme, it is called an *internal rhyme* or a *middle rhyme*.

RHYME SCHEMES

As we have seen in our analysis of the various song forms, lyricists most often create lyrics that have a distinct rhyme scheme. We use letters to identify the pattern of the rhymes in lines of lyrics. Lines with the same letters end with words that rhyme. Several rhyme schemes are possible.

Table 8: Possible Patterns for a Four-Line Lyric

Pattern
ABAB
AABB
AAAA
ABBA
AXAA
AXXA
XAXA

("X" is used here to indicate the absence of a rhyme)

FULL RHYMES

Full rhymes, also called *ordinary rhymes*, are two words or the final syllables of two words, that are sung or said exactly alike (Example 79). One-syllable words that rhyme sound exactly alike except for the initial consonant.

Example 79: Some Words That Rhyme

> Bracket/Jacket/ Packet
> Ice/Price/Nice/Dice
> Dagger/Swagger/Stagger
> Apprehend/Defend/Attend/Amend
> Mellow/Cello/Fellow/Yellow

HALF RHYMES

Songwriters sometimes find themselves in a creative situation where a full rhyme is just not possible. Instead, they fashion a *half rhyme* or *imperfect rhyme*. These word pairs almost rhyme, but really do not. Half rhymes (sometimes also called *slant rhymes*) are word pairs that end with the same consonant, but do not share the same preceding vowel sound. I believe that half rhymes are less good and are to be avoided in crafting your lyrics. The words *moon* and *run* do not rhyme; only their last consonants are the same. They are half rhymes when paired as a couplet, as are the words *bridge and grudge* and *self-assured* and *doors*. This last word pair, *self-assured* and *doors* are from the closing couplet of the Lennon and McCartney song, "Help!"

> But these days are gone, I'm not so self-assured,
> Now I find I've changed my mind, I've opened up the doors.

It is very hard to argue that the Beatles were at all injured using this near rhyme. But, it is the only couplet in the song that is not a full rhyme. Could Lennon or McCartney come up with a line that rhymes? Considering their vast output and masterworks like "Yesterday" and "Here There and Everywhere," it is likely they could. But, even in their seminal "Eleanor Rigby" there is a half rhyme:

> ...as he walks from the grave
> no one was saved.

Ah, the lovely lyrics. Where do they all belong?...No one is perfect, but I do like the challenge of making words work well. My advice: try to rhyme, unless you have Sir

George Martin producing your album and a company like EMI Records underwrites your project.

The words, *day* and *grey* are technically also considered half rhymes (at least in the British spelling of grey), since they are not spelled the same. For the purposes of song lyrics though, where it is the sound of things that matters, they are perfectly acceptable words to pair, as are *pack* and *maniac* and *pain* and *campaign*.

POLYSYLLABIC RHYMES

In *polysyllabic rhymes*, the last two or three syllables match exactly (Example 80). Words in this category include:

Example 80: Polysyllabic Rhymes

> elation/sensation
> intersection/affection
> feline/beeline/sealine
> addiction/benediction/affliction
> laborious/victorious
> sufficiency/deficiency

A special kind of invented polysyllabic rhyme can be found in the very old song, "I Can't Give You Anything But Love." In the first stanza of this 1928 tune by composer, Jimmy McHugh and lyricist, Dorothy Fields, Fields constructs a polysyllabic rhyme for the word, "Happiness" by rhyming it with a half rhyme on the "-i-" of "happiness" and a full rhyme on –ness:

> Dream a while…scheme a while
> You're sure to find…happiness and I guess…

Such an old song! "Why include it here as an example?" you ask. Because this relic from the roaring twenties was recorded so many times—we should all be so lucky—it deserves scrutiny. Most recently, "I Can't Give You Anything But Love" was included the album *Cheek to Cheek* (released in 2014), in a duet by Tony Bennett and Lady Gaga. Let's hope that one of your songs is still being recorded in eighty-six years!

ASSONANCE

The literary device known as *assonance* takes place when two words that are in close proximity share the same vowel sound, but start with different consonant sound. The repetition of vowel sounds can create internal rhyming within the line, as is the case with the words *reticence* and *penitence*.

The opening line of the song, "Everything Happens to Me," with music by Matt Dennis (1914-2002) and lyrics by Tom Adair (1913-1988), contains three words that create assonance:

"I make a date for golf and you can bet your life it rains."

The words, *make, date* and *rains* all have a long a sound. The assonance in this line helps make it memorable.

ALLITERATION

Alliteration is the same sound or letter at the beginning of adjacent or near each other. The quick succession of "b's" in the title hook of the song, "Bye, Bye Blackbird" with music by Ray Henderson (1896-1970, and lyrics by Mort Dixon (1892-1952) are alliterative as are the "l's" in the Bacharach and David song, "The Look of Love."

Exercises

Exercise #1

Create a syllable-by-syllable analysis of the lyrics for one of your favorite pop tunes by transcribing the lyrics onto a new sheet of paper. Place a hyphen between each multi-syllable word like this: Philadelphia would become, Phil-a-del-phi-a.

Using your syllabic analysis as a guide, create a new lyric with the same syllable count. For instance, Philadelphia has five syllables. It could be replaced by another five-syllable word or by a phrase like, "You and I are one."

Exercise #2

Use the lyric you created in Exercise 1 as the basis for a new song. I suggest you build your new song in a very different style, key and tempo as the original song you analyzed.

Exercise #3

Begin a list of potential song titles that incorporate alliteration as a key element, as does "Philadelphia Freedom," "Sexy Sadie," "Cuckoo Cocoon" and "Jumpin' Jack Flash."

Exercise #4

Begin a list of potential song titles that use colloquial expressions, like "Nine to Five," "I Got It Bad (And That Ain't Good)," and "One in a Million."

Exercise #5

Compose a story song.

Go somewhere public where you can observe people; a park, a train station, a museum, or a diner (I prefer "greasy spoons" for this exercise. Don't order more than coffee in consideration of your health, though). Sit. Watch. Listen. Learn.

Then, choose a person about whom to write. Next, write in prose about an imagined episode from your main character's life, past, present or future.

The next step is to reduce your story to a single thought that can become your title. See, at this point, if your prose story and title can inspire you to create a lyric and a tune or part of a lyric and tune.

CHAPTER SEVEN

REASONS TO WRITE... METHODS TO MONETIZE

The American composer, Ned Rorem, was once asked the question, "Why do I compose the way I do?" His reply was, "Why do I compose, period? Then he added:

> "Less from self-expression than because I want to be an audience to something that will satisfy me. The act dispels the smokescreen between my ego and reality. However my gifts may seem a luxury to others, I compose for my own necessity, because no one else makes quite the sound I wish to hear."

A REASON TO WRITE

Perhaps most of us who compose do so to fill a need we perceive. We want to hear certain music at a certain time, so we sing it into existence. The experience of singing music into existence often happens first in families. Parents and other adults sing songs to the children in their care to make mundane, everyday tasks feel special, to mark occasions like marriages, births and funerals, and to create and maintain traditions. Some of the songs that adults sing to kids are classic family songs, like the "Lullaby and Goodnight" ("Brahm's Lullaby"), or "Row, Row, Row Your Boat," but moms and dads also spontaneously make up the songs they sing to the children in their lives. Caretakers often accompany routine events like going to sleep with newly created tunes. Apparently, children learn this creative impulse quickly, as toddlers can readily be observed imitating their parents as they make up songs in play with their friends.

Researchers, like Dr. Lori A. Custodero of Teachers College at Columbia University in New York believe that parents across all cultures make expressive, nonverbal vocalizations to their children. Custodero observed that children respond in a similar manner completing a circuit that she says is often one of the first ways human beings relate to one another. She postulates that parents from all civilizations sing lullabies and other songs to their children and that children from all civilizations spontaneously make up songs as they play. It's easy to imagine that this song-creating urge began with our early ancestors thousands of years ago.

Songs That Fill a Void

Songs are composed for many purposes and are used in many ways. Certainly, at its core the need for humans to make music with their mouths probably has to do with our urge to tell people how we feel. Most of the songs we compose have lyrics that explain our feelings about something, be it a lover, a car, a political ideology, or a can of tuna fish.

Fame and Fortune

An obvious byproduct of composing a song that becomes hugely popular is the twin likelihood that the writer will become famous and make a lot of money. These lofty goals may very well be reasonable to some, but if this is the why behind your urge to make music, forget it. Consider seriously a career in hedge funds or speculative real estate development.

The truth is I have never met a hit-writing songwriter whose primary goal was to become rich and famous. Hit writers with whom I have worked, Eric Bazilian, William DeVaughn, Lzzy Hale, Robert Hazzard, Bobby Eli and Patti LaBelle, wrote songs because they liked to, were great at it and felt they had something to say in a unique way.

I do not mean here to imply that financial gain and notoriety is not desirable or that these very successful tunesmiths did not desire financial solvency. It is only that I believe success is measured in many ways; becoming rich and famous are but two.

Studying music, becoming proficient as a composer, performer, arranger or producer— or all of these—is a reward in itself. Learn about the business of music, too, and you might find that you can make a significant part of or all of a good income from your art. Pursuing any artistic expression for the cause of becoming wealthy is a fool's game that will yield massive frustration and likely result in your working in some other field anyway.

But financial success can happen.

You can write a song that becomes popular and that can lead to financial rewards. However, the surest way to succeed is to honor yourself and the art of music by becoming better than most at musical self-expression. Anything less is a get-rich-quick scheme.

End of sermon! Let's look at some of the ways people use songs.

COMMON AND NOVEL WAYS PEOPLE USE SONGS

Ask any ten folks on the street to define accomplishment in music and you will likely find that seven or eight of them will mention having a hit record as *the* measure of success. Popular culture, television and film, do little to dissuade people of this notion. Left out of films and television shows are stories of all the great musicians who work behind the scenes to help craft and polish aspiring writer's and artist's products. Similarly, the stories of the thousands of creative musicians who compose songs for other reasons than making a hit record are also not generally told. But the truth is that there are many excellent musicians who craft music that does not hit, and a lot of music that does hit is just plain awful.

In the early chapters of this book, I wrote about the how-to aspects of the craft of songwriting. For the remainder of this chapter, I will write about my strategies for entering, staying in and succeeding in the songwriting business. I will enumerate my suggestions for actions you can take to advance your career including my thoughts about how you can work to create opportunity, and become a part of a hit record project.

Now, go back and reread the last two sentences. These might be the most important words I have shared with you in this book.

The key words in those two sentences are songwriting business, opportunity, and project.

SONGWRITING AS A BUSINESS

Writing music just for the heck of it is a swell thing to do. I do it all the time. I have composed music with no clear business purpose for almost my entire life. I consider this practice for my work or a kind of entertainment for myself. Sometimes that kind of non-goal oriented writing project is for my own education as I experiment with a new technique to challenge myself. And sometimes the music that comes from these efforts finds its way into a commissioned project, sometimes not.

But here's the thing—unless you treat your composing as a business you will remain a hobbyist, and that is OK. Composing songs for fun is a very cool hobby to have, and it's a whole lot safer hobby than, say, jousting.

If you want to be in the music business, and specifically in the songwriting business, you must create a business model that includes keeping regular hours every day during which you write something, even if just for practice.

Writing every day is difficult. You will probably discover many reasons why you should do something else: Your shoes need polishing, your dishes need washing, or your significant other desires your undivided attention. You get the idea.

The truth is exercising your creative skills is like exercising your body's muscles. The more you do it, the more limber and strong you become.

You are probably thinking that what I am suggesting is an impossible thing, because you are not inspired everyday. So what? You were probably not very inspired to do your algebra homework either. You did it though. Songwriters who write only when inspired are uninspiring songwriters.

I have worked for a few of these want-to-be songwriters over my years in the music production business. If you are the kind of person who can only write when some major life event happens, fine. But that is like practicing your instrument only when you feel moved to do so. That is an OK attitude for a hobbyist, but not a very good or realistic business model for the aspiring professional. The model I am suggesting does not require that you lead a miserable life or an upbeat one, either. I only suggest that you spend a regular part of each day of the life you lead devoted to the creation of new songs.

NOT ALL WELL-WRITTEN SONGS ARE HITS. NOT ALL HITS ARE WELL-WRITTEN SONGS.

It is likely you already know these music industry truisms. You have written some songs you know are great or you know persons who have. Yet, these creations have somehow not won the acclaim you think they should. Similarly, you have heard recordings of poorly constructed songs that have become commercially successful.

It takes more than great musical and lyrical craftsmanship to cause a song to top the trade magazine charts.

Hit Songs Are the Products of the Music Industry

A hit song is the product of the music industry. It is the result of a successful collaborative effort of songwriters, record producers, recording engineers, musicians, singers, mastering engineers, record label executives, promotions persons, art directors, advertising professionals, broadcast professionals—and is immensely dependent upon luck.

Sometimes songs become successful because the highly competent persons who run the well-oiled music business machine use a technique called *push marketing*. A poorly written, poorly produced song can sometimes be made into a wildly successful product. The same is true of mediocre performers. While frustrating for the journeyman tunesmith, these occasional equivalents to the successful late night cable television product are a fact of music business life.

Publishers and Writers Earn Royalties

Later in this chapter I will discuss the various members of a songwriter's team. Perhaps the most important teammate a songwriter can have is a great publisher. A music publisher will provide the songwriter with the business wherewithal to get the songwriter's songs out to the public and will insure that the songwriter receives as much compensation as he can for his work. A great publisher is a songwriter's essential partner.

What is Music Publishing?

The chief business activities of music publishers are two: First, to exploit the *intellectual property* they own by seeking to have it performed, recorded and otherwise used by as many musicians as possible; And second, to collect fees for the use of their intellectual property and then to administer the distribution of those fees to the creators of the music. They get persons to use the music they own and they collect and distribute the money they earn from those uses.

WHAT IS BEING SOLD?
HOW IS A SONGWRITER PAID?

The product of an artistic endeavor is called intellectual property under the Copyright Law of the United States as contained in *Title 17 of the United States Code.* In the music business, songs and recordings are construed as intellectual property.

Like other kinds of property, intellectual property can be owned, sold, rented, stolen or given away.

MECHANICAL ROYALTIES

In 1917 several of the large and medium-sized publishers in New York City formed the National Music Publishers Association (NMPA). One of their chief tasks was to issue *mechanical licenses* for songwriters and publishers to those who wanted to record a song. A mechanical license is a special agreement that grants a record company permission to make a record.

The mechanical license is an agreement that spells out in clear terms, the use of the composition and the payments due for its use. Through this legal document, music publishers were able to derive a fee (called a *mechanical royalty*) for the use of their copyrights in recordings.

In 1927, the NMPA established the Harry Fox Agency (HFA) to manage this part of their work. The HFA is named after the man who became well known in his job with NMPA, as he was the person who doled out the mechanical licenses. Another company, Rightsflow®, was acquired by Google in 2011 to provide mechanical licenses and is a competitor of HFA.

PERFORMANCE ROYALTIES

Publishers and their composers established entities called *Performing Rights Organizations* (PROs) to collect and distribute fees called *performance royalties* for the performance of their songs.

Today, three organizations work on behalf of composers, lyricists and publishers to collect performance royalties. These are the American Society of Composers, Authors and Publishers (ASCAP), Broadcast Music Inc. (BMI) and SESAC (formerly, the Society of European Stage Authors and Composers, but now just SESAC). A performance royalty is paid to a song's publisher each time the song is played (or performed) on the radio, on television, on the Internet, or at a concert venue, club or restaurant.

As record companies grew more and more important, the symbiotic relationship between publishers and record companies also grew. The allegiances between music publishers and record companies survive to this day, however as I will explain below, the near-monopoly once held by large publishing houses and large record companies has been somewhat shattered by technological developments that began in the late Twentieth Century.

BECOMING KNOWN AS A SONGWRITER

As an aspiring music businessperson, you need to become known to others in the professional music business community. You will likely be surprised at how helpful others in the community will be; musicians are a very caring gaggle of folks, especially if you are talented and have a good attitude.

You can meet other like-minded musicians in lots of ways. For instance, you can make use of social networks like MeetUp, FaceBook and LinkedIn to join already established groups of musicians, songwriters and others interested in having a career in the music business.

When you qualify for membership, you can join The National Academy of Recording Arts and Sciences (The Recording Academy).

THE RECORDING ACADEMY®

The members of the Recording Academy are the top-notch recording industry professionals who are making hit records. The Recording Academy regularly schedules business/social events where you can meet members and other aspiring artists. They also sponsor educational workshops where you can learn new skills from experienced professionals at the peak of their powers.

ASCAP, SESAC and BMI, as well as groups like the Nashville Songwriters Association, also present educational workshops and open songwriter sessions where fellow aspirants and professional songwriters and can listen to your new songs and offer suggestions.

N S A I
"IT ALL BEGINS WITH A SONG"

As a member of your local community, you may also find it helpful to attend the meetings of groups like the Lions Club, the Rotary Club and the Chambers of Commerce. While much more of a long shot in terms of obtaining a direct assignment or even a direct connection, being known as a songwriter by members of these organizations could aid you in meeting others who share your passion and interest, or better yet, need your services. Being around and being known are necessary ingredients for opportunity, our next subject.

Opportunity

It is quite impossible to have success in anything without first having opportunity. You can't win if you are not permitted to play.

To me, opportunity, means both being permitted to participate and being equipped to contend. Success is about opportunity, and opportunity is something you make by staying observant, being around the action and being prepared.

Preparation comes from learning, researching, studying, and practicing your craft. (Hey, you bought this book—that is a very good start!). But there are other things.

There are other ways to learn and other things in music to study. Work with a great songwriting coach, take a class to study music theory with an inspiring and learned teacher, learn from a motivated educator how to play an instrument and how to sing—these are all terrific pursuits that will provide you powerful skills that will help propel you towards your goal of achieving success in the songwriting business.

Instrumentalists, please notice that I am suggesting that you learn how to sing in addition to learning to play your instrument. You don't have a great voice? No problem. Having a great voice is not a prerequisite. Having a good understanding of how singers make music, how ridiculously perilous it is to count on your voice as a tool, how remarkably easy it is to sing just a little flat or sharp—these are all things every musician, and especially every songwriter, should know at a visceral level.

Finding opportunities means staying observant. One is not helped by wearing blinders, by looking in only one direction to find places and persons who will want to make good use of your songwriting abilities. Opportunity often comes looking for you in the most common of places and for the most ordinary of reasons.

Your path to writing a hit song for the world's next big recording personality might just be through writing a song for a local stage production, even if you know nothing about theatre and were frightened by an actress as a small child. Your road to the Songwriter's Hall of Fame might first find you writing a fight song for a political candidate for whom you would never vote. Alternatively, your trail to triumph might include a detour to the land of radio spot advertising where you will write one of the world's best pieces of advertising music, even though you hate jingles and advertising, and are a devout Socialist.

I am not for a minute suggesting that you "sell out." How could I? I know not what this phrase means! What I am suggesting is that in my mind, to write is to write is to write. You do it because you are good at it, you need the practice, you want to work, you believe you compose with a unique voice and you want to see what new opportunities will come from taking advantage of the door that was opened for you.

All of the writing opportunities I have just described can be considered practice for the larger opportunity that may or may not come along. In the meantime, you are plying your craft and honing it while you do. But wait…did I just say that your big chance might or might not happen? Well, yes. Yes I did.

The unfortunate truth is that sometimes no matter how talented, methodical, well trained, persistent, kind, obedient, cheerful, thrifty, brave, clean and reverent—the top-tier chance for tremendous triumph takes a backseat to luck. Sometimes there is that, but mostly luck is opportunity of a different name.

PROJECTS

Music making is often a team sport. The obvious examples are bands, choirs and orchestras. There is also collaborative songwriting. Writing with another creative person can be an exhilarating and rewarding experience. It can just as often be a tedious and tantrum-filled exercise in frustration. I am confident that these will be self-limiting. All of the activities I have listed I see as projects.

WORK-FOR-HIRE

Sometimes songwriters are asked to provide their songs on a *work-for-hire* basis. In a work-for-hire arrangement, the songwriter gives up all future rights to additional income in consideration of a one-time payment upfront. Work-for-hire deals are usually the province of the beginner and are often a source of regret later in that writer's life.

Any of the business opportunities listed in the next section can be presented as a work-for-hire job. The talented aspiring songwriting professional needs to exercise tremendous patience and self-control when offered a work-for-hire opportunity since signing away all future rights and income based on your present efforts might be a choice you will regret later and for a very long time.

TOP USES FOR SONGS

What is it to be in the songwriting business? In its simplest incarnation, it is an exchange of goods for services where one person pays another to create an original song. Most of us want to be the writer of a song that becomes a classic for which we become well known and wealthy; there are other ways that songwriters can be paid for their creative efforts.

Here is my list of some of those ways. Some are obvious and well documented in the popular media. Several are less well known and might be a surprise for you.

Major Label Releases

Having a song released on a commercially distributed record *album* is one of the pinnacles of success in the songwriting business. It is even more thrilling if your song is chosen as a single, but either way, being part of a major label album release is a big deal opportunity. How does it pay? The present rate of payment for songs on albums, legislated by Congress, is 9.1¢ per song for each album sold. This is the mechanical royalty. The mechanical royalties ("the mechanicals") are split equally between the publisher and the writers. That means that the publisher and writers each receive half of $91.00, or $45.50 for every one hundred albums sold.

In addition to the mechanicals, songwriters (and their publishers) whose songs hit and receive radio, television and Internet play will earn performance royalties. Performance royalties are collected and distributed by ASCAP, BMI and SESAC. Writers whose songs are included in a major release album, but are not the hit single, will likely see little or no performance royalties. This is still lucrative and a big deal, since the savvy songwriter will promote the heck out of being on a hit album. They can leverage their connection to a hit album and a hit artist into other song placement opportunities. This is opportunity knocking hard on your door. Listen and open the door.

Dance School Albums

Smart songwriters often look for less obvious opportunities to practice their trade. Most of the less obvious opportunities can be found in businesses that need music, but market to a smaller segments of the population than does the commercial record industry.

These may not be the hit record opportunity that you pine for, but they are real opportunities to have your music performed and recorded and for you to be paid. They will provide you practice, income, experience and exposure.

Albums of music specially tailored for the needs of dance schools and dance instructors represent a very small portion of the total sales of record albums. There are hundreds of dance schools around the country. All use music to teach ballet, jazz, hip-hop and ballroom dances. Many dance schools use albums that are specially produced to fulfill the educational needs of dance instructors.

Songwriters will derive income from mechanical royalties at the same payment rate as paid for commercially released mass-market albums. However, since per-album sales are limited, composers often push for significant upfront payments. Songwriters who write for dance school albums might receive performance royalties, since many dance schools are signatories to an agreement with ASCAP, BMI or SESAC.

Performance royalties from anything other than the repeated broadcast of a hit record will be small or non-existent, but diligent songwriting professionals can report in-school use of their compositions to their PRO. Albums from small labels, like The Ballet Dance Company, populate the music-for-dance-class market. For more information about music created especially for dance classes, go to DanceClassMusic.com. There you can find the names of labels you can contact about having them record your songs for their albums.

Production Music Libraries

Production Music Library companies create tracks that are licensed exclusively for use as background music in broadcast commercials, television programs, educational, motivational, and corporate films. They are not licensed for entertainment like commercially released recordings.

Production music library companies are always in need of new material, but most of what they need is instrumental music and they will usually want their acquisitions to be in the form of a master-quality recording. This means that unless you are an experienced producer and arranger, you will need to hire someone to arrange your music and make your recording.

Production music library companies generally function as small record labels, but rather than market their wares to the general population, they market exclusively and directly to radio stations, television stations, networks, audio, and video and film producers.

Because music library compositions are licensed strictly for use as soundtracks for other audio and visual productions, you should not expect a hit record-like income from any piece you license to these companies, but you will be paid. Here is how.

Production music library companies function on a few different levels and adhere to a few different business models. The largest companies are often part of a large jingle production company. These businesses, like FirstCom Music and Killer Tracks, will employ a staff of composers, arrangers and producers to create their new albums. Staff composers are salaried. They will often not receive a share of synchronization or mechanical royalties, but may receive performance royalties through their PRO.

Synchronization royalties are paid when a piece of music is synchronized with the moving image of a film. Synchronization (or synch) fees vary greatly from production to production. The larger production music library companies provide commercial, television and film producers and others with synchronization licenses for the use of their productions and composition in their productions. The synch fee is dependent on the type of use and may range from around $100 for the use of a composition in a locally-played radio commercial, to several thousand dollars for the synch of a piece in a feature film.

Some larger music library companies, including NonStop Music (owned by Warner/Chappel Publishing) and Hens Teeth Music of Australia pay songwriters and producers a split of derived income from synchronization.

Other smaller production music library companies like AirCraft Music Library and Prolific Arts Music use a *buyout* music library model. In this scenario, all end users pay the same amount to purchase the rights to use a track in any way they would like, for as long as they like.

Buyout music library companies are often owned and operated by composers and producers who also create the majority of the library's tracks. However, because libraries need so many tracks to fill their catalog's and their client's needs, many contract with independent producers and composers from whom they acquire tracks.

A songwriter desirous of working with this kind of music library company will need to compose instrumental pieces and cause them to be fully produced, either undertaking the production herself or contracting it out to a professional producer.

A songwriter with a fully produced instrumental track of her song can expect to receive an advance against royalties of $200 to $1,000 from a music library publisher. This could yield additional royalties or be a work-for-hire agreement that will pay nothing additional.

BROADCAST COMMERCIALS

Another great place where songwriters can work and get paid well is in the music for advertising business. Today, the fields of music for advertising now also includes composing new music for website and for advertising on the Internet, and can also occasionally include composing a special advertising song for an in-store kiosk or other display.

Jingle production houses are often associated with production music library companies, and exist on a few levels: There are companies that produce locally played or regionally played jingles, and those that produce jingles that accompany television and radio advertising that plays nationally. Many medium-sized cities have at least one jingle company that produces local jingles and the occasional regional spot. The nationally aired commercials are mostly produced in New York, Los Angeles, Chicago, Nashville and Dallas.

The larger jingle production companies, for instance Tuesday Productions and Jam Creative Productions, Inc., employ a staff of songwriters, composers, producers, and arrangers who crank out radio and television jingles daily. These salaried employees retain no ownership in their creations, working on a work-for-hire basis. Songwriters in this field can receive performance royalties for their broadcast jingles, but these are usually quite inconsequential or nonexistent.

An adjunct to the large jingle producer's business is the *radio station id* package. These are the very short *shotgun* announcements and *sweepers* that one hears on pop radio that sing the name of the station. They will often be created in the style of the music the station plays. Songwriters who create these products are part of the company's salaried staff and will receive no additional payments, including performance royalties.

Many jingles are produced by one-person shops and are made on a buyout basis with no additional payments ever made to the songwriter. Songwriters who work in these smallest of the small jingle shops are often well-qualified audio producers, instrumentalists and singers, or partners with some other music-type who is. Folks who produce in this business model can expect to create local jingles and receive from $1,000 to $5,000 for each jingle production. From this, they will need to pay for studio, musicians and singers. Generally, this kind of buyout business arrangement yields no performance royalty on the backend.

ANTHEMS

Corporations and sports teams sometimes hire songwriters to create a song for the launch of a particular product or campaign. This kind of *anthem* can be is similar in spirit to a national anthem, but will usually be in a contemporary style. Lee Greenwood's "Proud to be an American" is the model here.

Corporate and sports team anthems are usually produced by jingle production companies as an adjunct to their other work, since they are in fact long form jingles.

EDUCATIONAL AND CHILDREN'S ALBUMS

Popular recording artists from Johnny Cash to Def Leppard have made recordings of songs written especially for children. Other songwriters and recording artist who specialize in creating music for young children include Raffi, Miss Amy and Brady Rymer.

Some of these artists have successfully established specialized record labels and publishing companies to support their artistic endeavors as writers and performers.

Several larger companies also specialize in creating recordings (and videos) for children. Companies including, Kidz Bop, Veggie Tales, The Disney Company and Sesame Workshop operate as specialized record labels and publishers. They employ a staff of songwriters and producers to make their recordings that are especially tailored to fill the needs of young children (and their parents).

Musical Theater

Like the music business in general, most "civilians" (those who are not involved in the trenches of the music business) have a very narrow view of musical theater. In the minds of most, musical theater exists exclusively in Manhattan and London. It does not! *Musicals* are performed all over the world, all the time. What is more, they are regularly created and performed by writers and performers who are not at all famous.

Like hit records and getting a song in a movie soundtrack, being part of a Broadway show is about as good as it gets. And at any given time there are perhaps twenty songwriters whose songs are being belted out in America's *Great White Way*. So, for the rest of us, there are options. These include writing shows especially for performances in high schools, middle schools and community theater.

Successful composers on Broadway usually negotiate individual agreements with producers that allow the producers to use the music in their shows. Once a show has had a successful run on Broadway, the producers will allow it to be mounted in other cities, in smaller theaters and for shorter runs. In return, the producers will be paid a fee by the local theater impresario. These fees are termed *grand rights*. Grand rights royalties are split between the show's original producers, the songwriters and perhaps some others involved in the creation of the show. The precise royalty and the proportions of the split are negotiable. Once agreed to, the amounts are memorialized in the production agreement.

If a cast album of the music is produced, or other well-known artists produce new recordings of the songs from the show, the show's music publisher and the writers divide the mechanical and performance royalties in the usually 50/50 split. If a film version of the show is created, the publishers and writers divide the synchronization royalties equally.

It is an expensive matter to pay the grand rights to produce a famous musical. Often these fees are deemed too costly for a school to pay. Schools may opt instead to mount productions of shows that are not at all well known. The shows are written by little known songwriters and published by companies including: Pioneer Drama Service, Musicline School Musicals and ArtReach Children's Theater Plays. The publishers of school musicals generally charge the presenters (the school) a performance royalty for each performance they present. These fees ($45 to $75 per show) are divided in some proportion between the publisher and the writers based on the songwriter's negotiating skills and stature.

Choir Music

There are many publishers of music for choirs. *Choir music* publishers like Alfred Music, Hal Leonard, Shawnee Press and Carl Fischer Music publish both secular and sacred music. Other publishers, like Augsburg Fortress, GIA and Morningstar Music Publishers specialize in music for the church.

Publishers of choral music release their publications in print and in demonstration recordings. Choral publishers are always looking for newly created songs, however they must be arranged for choir: They must be written in standard choir configurations in two, three or four parts (female and male; soprano I, soprano II and alto; or soprano, alto, tenor, bass). Songwriters who are skilled with this kind of part writing can expect to earn about 10% of the retail price of each printed copy sold. They will also collect performance royalties from ASCAP, BMI or SESAC for performances of their pieces.

Background Environmental Music

Have you ever had the experience of walking into a clothing store or through a shopping mall where every step you take is accompanied by a great sounding recording you never before heard?

The background music you are hearing as you shop is called *environmental music*. It is written and recorded by independent songwriters and producers and licensed for use in businesses by companies like Muzak and DMX. These companies also supply background music-on-hold, scent and other marketing services to a variety of businesses in the healthcare, retail and hospitality industries.

Muzak, DMX and other companies in the background music business acquire master-quality recordings for their catalog from independent songwriters and producers. Interestingly, the music that environmental music companies license can be in almost any musical style, from dance, to polka; folk-rock to classical; instrumental and vocal.

These kinds of companies function as publishers and pay writers and other copyright owners a mechanical and performance royalty based on the number of installations that play the writer's track and the number of times it is played. Like many opportunities in the songwriting and recording business, producing music for use in business as background is a numbers game because each use pays very little per use. One needs many songs being used in many locations to derive a reasonable revenue.

Agreements with environmental music suppliers like Muzak are usually non-exclusive. A songwriter can therefore license her music to another publisher for some other use, in addition to its use as background business music.

Songs are created for use as recorded entertainment, film and television themes and underscoring. They are also recorded to motivate people (as in national anthems, corporate anthems and commercial jingles). They are used for education (songs that teach, like the "Baa, Baa, Black Sheep," "Fifty, Nifty United States" or hymn tunes used to teach the verses of the Bible), for stage performance (like operas or Broadway-style shows), and for religious and secular print publishing (the music written especially for use by school and community choirs).

YOUR WORK RECORDED AND PUBLISHED

Once we have completed our creation, and we are convinced we have tweaked and polished our diminutive masterwork beyond all second-guessing, what do we do with it?

If you are a member of a band, you bring your new song to your next band rehearsal and try to convince the rest of the band that this is the tune that will win you the record business lottery.

If you are a choir director at a house of worship, or a music therapist, you bring your tune in to the next rehearsal or meeting and teach it to your constituents.

There are options beyond the personal connections or needs you might have in your music-related work. These are publishing and recording. These are two distinct music business endeavors that are more than ever very closely intertwined.

MUSIC PUBLISHING AND THE RECORDING INDUSTRY

Beginning in 1501 when Ottaviano Petrucci (1466-1539) of Venice published the *Harmonice musices odhecaton*, the first collection printed entirely from movable type, and lasting through about the mid-1990s, the business of publishing music was limited to firms that were substantially capitalized.

Music publishing and printing was a very expensive proposition. Publishers needed to purchase and maintain the music typesetting machines and large printing presses. They needed to hire the expert tradespersons and musicians who could edit, arrange and typeset music and run the complicated gear. Moreover, in later centuries, music publishers needed to employ a sizable staff of administrators, graphic designers and marketing experts.

The print music publishing business began to change in the 1960s when the Xerox Corporation of Rochester New York introduced the first dry paper copiers, making it a bit less costly for start-up music publishers to enter the market.

PUBLISHING JOINS RECORDING

Up until the invention of the gramophone by Thomas Edison in 1877, music publishers were almost exclusively concerned with creating and marketing music in print (although, from the late nineteenth century through the mid-1920s, a small part of publisher's revenues came from the production of rolls for player pianos). As the popularity of record players increased and the popularity of the parlor piano and the sheet music to play on it waned, music publisher's goals shifted from music printing towards records. Having their titles recorded became an important and increasingly profitable pursuit.

RECORDS ADVERTISE PUBLISHER'S SONGS

The early part of the Twentieth Century was also a time when broadcast radio gained in reliability and popularity. Publishers quickly grasped the vast potential causing recordings of their songs to be produced. Radio could now advertise their songs. Publishers who had once relied on song pluggers to demonstrate their songs in department stores now heard their products introduced to the public at little or no cost to them.

Realizing that recordings could not exist without the intellectual property they controlled, publishers were soon able to convince their collaborators in the burgeoning record industry to pay for the privilege of recording their songs.

MUSIC PUBLISHING AND THE FILM INDUSTRY

Beginning in the earliest days of sound with film, with the release in 1927 by Warner Brothers of the film, *The Jazz Singer*, filmmakers have included music as a necessary part of their productions. Today, film companies including Walt Disney Studios, Twentieth Century Fox, Warner Brothers and Sony Pictures Entertainment, each have music publishing subsidiaries with whom their producers closely work.

Producers use songs as an adjunct to the instrumental musical underscore that always accompanies the action of theatrical, educational and documentary films. Songs may appear as the theme song for the film, as part of the underscore, or as a *diegetic* sound element, as source music. Source music is the music you hear in a film that appears to be coming from a radio or from a band playing on-camera. Having one of your songs included as part of a film's soundtrack is one of a songwriter's most lucrative and major accomplishments. It is certainly well worth the effort, but how does it happen? How does a songwriter have her song even considered for inclusion in a film?

I spoke with film composer Joe Renzetti about how an aspiring songwriter might get a song into a film. Renzetti, who earned an Academy Award in 1973 for his score for *The Buddy Holly Story*, provided this insight:

> "The very best way to have a song become part of a theatrical film is to somehow be known to the music supervisor or, better yet, the director. Being there and being known to the decision makers is the best method.

> "The next best thing is to be a known commodity when the production team becomes stuck. A song might have been written for the film project, but at the last minute, perhaps during the mix session, the director decides it's just not quite right. Someone in the team knows you to be person who can quickly deliver and, voilá! All of a sudden, your song is part of a major film sound track!

> "Having a great reputation as a songwriter who can quickly and successfully create a song that well fits the needs of the film's producers might come as the result of networking and you having had even moderate success in an allied field, like having had a hit record, or having written for television or a high-profile music library.

> "Finally, getting your songs to filmmakers is one of the jobs of a good music publisher; maybe it's their most important job, because having a song in a film can lead to notoriety and income in so many other parts of the music industry."

Most large publishers, especially those directly connected with film studios; market their songwriter's songs to filmmakers. Some publishing companies specialize in securing synch licenses for their writers. I list a few of the important one in "Step A: If You Are" under "Recipes for Success" below.

A New Paradigm

Like producing high-quality printed music, it was a very costly endeavor to produce great-sounding recordings during most of the Twentieth Century. Professional multi-track recording studios were very expensive to rent and even more expensive to own and maintain. Add to that, the fees for expert professional studio musicians, arrangers, copyists, conductors, and producers and you have a process only a large corporation or the occasional well-heeled person could undertake.

And if you wanted to sell your record to recoup your investment you would need to add the cost of manufacturing long-playing records (LPs), 45 r.p.m records (45s) and cassette tapes. These delicate pieces of plastic (they were readily prone to spoilage due to a bit of heat) needed to be warehoused. Then, they needed to be distributed to retail stores, promoted to radio stations and otherwise advertised to the public.

The mid-century paradigm also dictated that record companies were usually responsible for the costs related to the development of young recording artists. Artist development costs could include the cost of grooming and the creation of an image, and fees for vocal coaches, speech coaches, academic tutors and a wardrobe.

Small record labels were generally too undercapitalized to be more than marginally successful (usually only on a regional basis) or aligned themselves with a larger corporation that would handle pressing, distribution and marketing. In these instances, the small label would cultivate the artist, find and produce the song and turn the master over to the major label with the sincere hope that their record would not be forgotten in the promotion man's piles of 45's.

The business model of the music publishing industry and record industry was forever changed during the late 1980s and 1990s when scientists developed the personal computer. Computer music sequencing, digital audio recording and the Internet all arrived shortly thereafter. These technological developments were the harbingers of what I call the democratization of the music industry. No longer would great recordings be produced only in the music capitals of New York, Los Angeles and Nashville. Now, almost anyone anywhere could make a recording whose audio fidelity rivaled that achieved in the most elaborate professional studios anywhere in the world. Moreover, distribution and promotion, the twin obstacles of success in the record industry for smaller independent producers, were largely torn down with the founding of CDNow, N2K, Music Boulevard and their successors TuneCore, The Orchard, CDBaby, iTunes and Amazon for distribution and FaceBook, YouTube and Vimeo for promotion.

The good news is that the cost of admission has been lowered; anyone who wants to produce and market a recording can. The bad news is that the cost of admission has been lowered; anyone who wants to produce and market a recording can.

This means good things for serious-minded and seriously talented musical artists. It also means that there is a whole lot of ear pollution caused by not-so-hot records on the Internet.

The basics remain; one needs a great song recorded in a great performance to make a hit record. In addition, one needs a better than average understanding of marketing and business to achieve record business success, especially trying to do it yourself.

The ease of access to the dream of music business stardom also provides a large pool of candidates for thieves and swindlers who would take advantage of all those starry-eyed folks. More than ever, those desiring a career in the music business are best served by collaborating with an expert who has many times navigated the waters of record production, pressing, distribution and promotion. To avoid the clutches of those dastardly miscreants who would take advantage of you at the first opportunity, consult with a qualified and respected record business professional about your music business goals. If you were building a house, you would hire a credentialed architect and a licensed builder.

Your music business career is no less important. Finding that well qualified expert who will treat your aspirations with care can be difficult. Ask others in your community who are in the music business, visit regional music conferences and attend the workshops and educational outreach programs presented by ASCAP, BMI, SESAC and the Recording Academy. Speak with the presenters at these events and ask them to recommend professionals in your region who can make great recordings and leave you with all five fingers when you shake hands.

The Cast of Characters

Success in the songwriting business requires that you interact with many music business folks. Surrounding yourself with a team of likeminded, goal oriented folks will help insure that you have a better than average chance to present your music to the public and have it provide a return on your investment of time and money.

Building Your Team

Developing a project around the process of making a commercial recording requires the collaboration of many highly skilled music professionals. At the least, this will include a recording artist, an engineer and a songwriter. There are often others: musicians, an arranger, a producer, back-up singers, perhaps a copyist, a musical contractor and a conductor.

Furthering your songwriting career will also require that you assemble a team of professionals who are expert in the business of music. This will probably include a music business lawyer, an accountant and perhaps a social media consultant, a website designer, a marketing specialist and a driver (Just kidding about the driver. Wait for that until you have your first or second hit record.).

The important message here is that success in the music business occurs for the individual when he or she is working in league with other creative, entrepreneurial persons, has prepared by learning at the feet of master practitioners, has tremendous tenacity, resilience and personal determination and seizes each new opportunity as if it is the opportunity of a lifetime.

Professional Manager

A professional manager is a salaried employee of a music publishing company. The professional manager is also sometimes called by the older title of song plugger.

This employee has two major functions: First, the professional manager is responsible for acquiring new songs for the publisher's catalog; second, he or she is responsible for causing those songs to be recorded by major recording artists.

To find new songs, the professional manager will review demonstration recordings, listen to performers at clubs and in-concert and generally stay aware of new folks making good music. In his role as a song plugger, the professional manager will send well-made demonstration recordings to all the artists he has on his personal contact list who he believes are good candidates for the tune. A great professional manager always has an ear open listening for new potential hit songs and remains aware of artist's recording schedules and tastes.

The professional manager can be your key contact person at a publishing company and is the person to whom you need to send your new songs.

Musical Arranger

An arranger is a highly skilled, creative musician who is expert in taking an existing piece of music (usually written by another person) and recasting it into a new and unique musical form. Arrangers are experts in the skill of orchestration and are usually conversant in many musical styles. Great arrangers can create a work in the style of Johann Sebastian Bach as easily as they can one in the style of Henry Mancini, Nelson Riddle or the Black Crows.

SONG DOCTOR

A song doctor is a musical specialist who works with songwriters to help them make their songs better crafted. Song doctors are part editor, part coach and cheerleader. A great song doctor will be conversant with the styles of many historical songwriters and will keep up-to-date on what is current in the recording and songwriting business. Record producers often wear the hat of song doctor for their artists.

STUDIO SINGER

Studio singers are highly skilled professionals who can blend well with other singers, generously take direction from conductors and producers, read music, sing in-tune and in time, learn very quickly and adapt to quickly changing expectations from the production team.

Studio singers come in two versions: One, the singer who can easily give over her individual vocal personality in favor of blending with a group; Two, singers with "character voices." These are persons with vast musical gifts whom, but for ambition, luck or looks could easily be the voice on a hit record.

STUDIO MUSICIAN

Recording studio musicians are highly skilled professionals who can work well with other musicians, generously take direction from conductors and producers, read music very, very well, and play in many different musical styles. Some studio musicians are equally comfortable working as soloists and in ensembles.

Studio players are paid well for their services and work within the strictures of the American Federation of Musicians' recording studio wage agreements.

The AFM is the musicians union. It was founded in 1896 to protect the rights and dignity of the highly skilled musical experts who perform at the industry's very highest standards. Although weakened significantly in recent years, the AFM remains an important player in the work of the most accomplished musicians in the country.

MUSICAL COPYIST

A musical copyist is a musical professional who is highly skilled in the preparation of sheet music parts for the recording ensemble (or live orchestra, choir or band). Copyists need to be good musicians and editors since they are required to catch the few errors that arrangers make. Copyists are aware of historically correct practices in musical notation and are expert users of the latest music publishing software. Great, old school copyists can quickly and accurately copy out parts by hand from a score using a special calligraphy pen and special India ink...just in case the computer dies or something needs to be fixed on the spot.

CONDUCTOR

A musical conductor is a very highly skilled, creative musician who directs an ensemble of musicians in a performance. Most conductors have superlative music reading skills, highly acute hearing (they can hear minor imperfections in professional musicians' tuning and timing) and have a very refined understanding of various musical styles. Conductors use their highly refined musical understanding and excellent communication skills to work with musicians to create with the musicians an outstanding musical performance.

MUSICAL CONTRACTOR

A musical contractor is a person who makes hiring decisions regarding the personnel for recording sessions, film and television soundtrack recordings, orchestral performances and stage show productions.

Contractors are usually professional musicians who are aware of the very best performing musicians in the area and who know the work rules the American Federation of Musicians (AFM) has in place regarding each work situation.

RECORD PRODUCER

A record producer wears many hats during the production of a song. The record producer is the key person who is ultimately responsible for the outcome of the efforts of the entire production team.

The most important responsibility of a record producer is to envision a sound for the song that he is producing. No matter what is the sound of the raw version of the song, the producer must imagine the entire collection of sonic elements that will make up the final production. The sonic elements of the final production will include its musical style, instrumentation, tempo, groove (or feel), voice type and so on.

Several things will influence a producer's imaginings about how she will produce a song. These will include Budget (can she hire thirty musicians or three?); the established image of the featured artist (is this a famous artist who has her own "sound"?); and finally, the imaginings of the other stakeholders (how would the record company executive or executive producer like the recording to sound?).

In order to bring her ideas to life, the record producer will next have to assemble the team. She will need to determine from her vast experience just which arranger is the right one, what musicians can best play in the style she is imagining, what studio and engineer will get the best sound for the project, and what mastering engineer can best polish the recording she has produced without compromising her production. Because a record producer is also the fiduciary responsible for working within a budget, she will make all personnel decisions with one eye on the costs. The producer is responsible for making sure the budget is not squandered. (The Christopher Guest character in *This is Spinal Tap* comes to mind.)

After the producer has firmly established her vision for the production, once all the musical artists are hired and the crew is working in the studio, the producer's job becomes one of quality control. Because the producer is at all times the singular person responsible for the sound of the recording, he or she must have the final word about how the music is recorded and performed. The producer is a cheerleader, psychologist to the performers, musical conductor, song doctor and quality control agent—all rolled into one. The producer must be able to hear the most minor of musical blemishes and clearly instruct the performer about how to remedy the problem, all without ruffling any sensitive artist's feathers.

The record producer sits alongside the mix engineer and the mastering engineer and guides each through the final stages of the recording process, at all times making certain that his or her vision of the recording comes to fruition.

Once the recording has been mixed and then mastered, the producer's job may be done. But depending on the status of the producer and the business arrangement he has established with the artist and other stakeholders, the producer might be involved in licensing the master recording and overseeing its manufacturing and distribution.

RECIPES FOR SUCCESS

In this text, I have thus far provided you with the basic materials of music, discussed lyric writing and several song forms and presented an overview of the music publishing and recording industries.

In the next section, I present for the writer who wants more than a hobby, a step-by-step how-to, a roadmap that you can follow to take you from song idea to getting your song used and getting paid.

- Come up with a hit song hook line that is accompanied by a musical motive that everyone will remember.
- Write the remainder of the song, first deciding in what form the song will be composed.
- Once your song complete—if you write with a co-writer(s), have him or her sign a split agreement that in simple language states who wrote what percentage of each part of the song. See sample split agreement in Example 81.

Example 81: Sample split agreement

Split Agreement for Music and Lyrics

15 January 2014

Our signatures at the foot of this document will confirm our complete understanding regarding a song now entitled, "This is a Bunny."

Be it known that, Johnny B. Great, wrote the music for "This is a Bunny" and that Sally Z. Swell, wrote the lyrics for "This is a Bunny."

Signed and dated:

_____   Date_____
Johnny B. Great

_____   Date_____
Sally Z. Swell

Great & Swell Songs
246 Justa Road
Someplace, TN 08882

Proceed to "Step A: If You Are Self-Publishing" or "Step B: If you Want to be Represented by a Major Publishing Company" below.

STEP A: IF YOU ARE SELF-PUBLISHING

If you are not immediately able to convince a major publishing company and record company that you are their next hit machine, and you believe in yourself enough to treat your career like a business and if you have the time and financial wherewithal to make the investments, you may choose to establish your own publishing company. In today's marketplace, that really means that you will establish yourself as a publishing company and a record label. Now, more than ever, easy access to the distribution and promotions platforms offered on the Internet allow all dedicated music business aspirants to establish themselves as independent music content providers.

Here is one man's recipe for do-it-yourself success in the music business.

HIRE A PRODUCTION TEAM TO MAKE A "RADIO READY" RECORDING OF YOUR SONG.

To have a "radio-ready" recording means to have a potential hit song that is represented in a recorded performance that compares well with anything one might hear on a radio station that plays music in the style of the recording. This means that you must have a singer with a hit record voice, a killer musical arrangement and great performances by fantastic musicians. Oh, and it needs to be a great recording, too!

Unless you are an experienced record producer, you will seriously need to consider hiring someone who has substantial record production credentials. If you live in one of the top twelve music business cities in the United States (Atlanta, Chicago, Miami/Orlando, Los Angeles, Memphis, Nashville, New York, Seattle, Washington/Portland Oregon, Philadelphia, Dallas/Huston, or Washington, D.C.), it will likely be an easy matter to ask around and find an experienced producer who you can hire. You may choose to contact the Recording Academy chapter in one of the top twelve cities near you for a few recommendations. You can learn more about the Recording Academy at www.grammypro.com.

Hiring an experienced record producer will insure that you will have top-notch musicians and singers on your session and that your song will be recorded at a fine studio with a great recordist.

REGISTER YOUR CLAIM IN COPYRIGHT

Once the master-quality recoding is complete, register you claim in copyright electronically by sending the application and an audio file of the recording along with a payment to www.copyright.gov. File a Form PA and a Form SR application so that you are copyrighting both the recording and the song that is embodied in the recording. Once you do, you will now be able to place the © and ⃞ symbols on any copies you release and your music, lyrics and your recording of your song will be protected from plagiarism. To be clear, someone can still plagiarize your work, but if it is copyrighted, you will have an easier time proving that you created it since what you are doing when you copyright a song is registering your claim of ownership with the Library of Congress.

As the creator of the musical work, you will also be provided certain assurances and guarantees under the Copyright Law. These include the right to make the first recording of the work, the right to license the work to others to perform, to print, to distribute and otherwise publish. Because of the Law, you can derive a fee from persons or companies that what to record your song, or publish it in print.

Under the present law, copyright protection begins as soon as the composer and lyricist fix their creation in some tangible form of expression (as soon as they write it down on paper or make a simple recording of the), and remains in force for the lifetime of the creators, plus seventy years after the last surviving author dies.

When you register your claim with the Library of Congress, you are simply putting the rest of the world on notice that this is, indeed, your creation. This is an incredibly important thing to do.

billboard

As a young songwriter, record producer and arranger, I had the good fortune of writing and producing a song that became a regional hit in the dance clubs and that was charted in *Billboard Magazine*. It was on a very small record label and we all did a very poor job of filing the appropriate papers and signing the appropriate contracts.

Many years later, I was approached by a European record company about having this production rereleased as part of a compilation record. I then spent the next nine months or so tracking down all of the important persons who were involved in this small label release. I did it, but it certainly would have been infinitely easier had I taken the time to invest in the minimal work of having an agreement with my co-writer.

Release Your Master Recording

Next, simultaneously release your master recording to online music stores and streaming services worldwide by contracting with a digital content aggregator like CDBaby or TuneCore. Doing this will place your great recording of your hit song for sale across the world via digital stores like iTunes, Amazon, Google Play and Spotify.

Digital content aggregators will usually provide an option to have your music distributed to satellite radio services like, Sirius XM and 1WorldSpace. Although the royalties from play on satellite radio are very small, you might well consider doing this. Think of this as advertising you do not need to pay for out-of-pocket. (You are paying, though, since you will not derive great direct financial benefit.)

Place a Video of Your Recording on YouTube, Vimeo or Instagram

Your video can be as elaborate or homespun as you like. The important thing is to have a version of the recorded version of your song on the Internet. Be sure to include a method for viewers to purchase your recording. Build a "call to action" into your video that will redirect prospects to iTunes or one of the other online outlets. Again, the royalties paid for having your music played on YouTube are paltry or nonexistent, but the advertising is worth it. You never know who is looking at these videos!

FORM YOUR OWN RECORD LABEL AND PUBLISHING COMPANY

Once you have a recording that is well produced and sounds like it could be played on the radio, you may want to speak with the program directors or music directors of stations in your hometown to see if they might air it. Having a record played on the traditional radio stations remains an important goal for recording artists and songwriters for a few reasons. Securing airplay helps to establish your brand and your credibility. Radio airplay is essentially free advertising that helps educate listeners about your product and might induce them to buy it. Having your record broadcast over the air and on Internet radio stations generates performance royalties through ASCAP, BMI or SESAC.

To generate the maximum revenue for your efforts in getting your record played, you can create a publishing company and become a publisher member of one of the PROs. By being both a publisher member and a writer member of a PRO, you can receive all the royalties generated from broadcast performances, and other performances, too.

Establishing yourself as a publisher is a simple process. To begin, look at the website of your PRO. There you will find step-by-step instructions. Next, you will need to check with your state to learn how to register the factious name of your new publishing company. It is always advisable to speak with the elders of your music community, to an attorney and possibly an accountant to learn how best to set up your new venture.

PROMOTE YOUR RECORDING TO RADIO STATIONS

As you can imagine, getting a top-tier radio station to play your record is like getting a date with a movie star. It might happen, but it is more likely to occur if you meet certain special criteria. For the major broadcasters in any size city, the principal criterion is that your song is recorded and released through a major record label.

As of 2011, there were more than fourteen thousand radio stations in the United States. Of these, the biggest stations in any town, the ones whose formats include Adult Contemporary (AC), Hot Adult Contemporary (Hot AC), Contemporary Hit Radio (CHR), Active Rock, Pop and Urban are generally only accessible to the machinery of the major record labels. The promotion teams of the major labels have well-oiled relationships with the big radio stations. Even with that, not everything promoted to a station by a record company promoter receives airplay, although it will probably be auditioned.

The stations that are available to independent artists and independent record labels include those with the Adult Album Alternative (AAA) format and college radio stations. Airplay on these stations can yield record sales and performance royalties and, with a little extra work, you might be able to arrange for performances at venues near the stations and colleges.

Begin by assembling a list of stations that are likely to be responsive to your request for airplay. Next, determine the correct person with whom to speak. This will usually be a person with the title, program director or music director. At some smaller stations, you might do well to contact the disc jockeys directly.

If you succeed in cultivating airplay on the more accessible stations and you create a "buzz" about your recording, you might be able to convince the program director or music director at a big station to audition your music. You can also report your any success you achieve to record companies if you decide to pursue a major label record deal.

Internet radio stations like Pandora and Spotify have become increasingly popular, while simultaneously hurting record and download sales. And, Internet play pays a much smaller performance royalty than does broadcast airplay. Nevertheless, for the independent recording artist and her record label Internet play might help generate interest in the music.

Being played on one of the many small Internet stations is of less significance. There are so many stations, each with such a small audience, each playing such a diversity selection of titles that the impact is not very potent.

JOIN A PERFORMING RIGHTS ORGANIZATION

Register yourself as a writer and your company as a publisher with Performing Rights Organization (PROs). There are three PROs in the United States, ASCAP, BMI or SESAC. PROs collect performance license fees from venues and broadcasters for all public performances at their establishments of music represented by the PRO. The PROs consider a public performance to either one that occurs in a public place or any place where people gather (other than a small circle of a family or its social acquaintances). They also consider a public performance to be one that is transmitted to the public. In this definition, a public performance also includes music played on radio or television broadcasts, music-on-hold, cable television and by the Internet.

Each PRO lumps together the performance fees they collect into one big pile of and then divvies up the money amongst its publisher members. Each PRO has its own formula for how they split the performance license fees up, but in a general way each publisher member receives a small payment for each time a piece of music they publish is reported as having been performed.

The performances are weighted; some are paid at a higher rate than are others. A performance by an orchestra at Carnegie Hall in New York City of a long symphonic work is paid at a higher rate than is the playing of a sixty-second jingle that airs on a 500-watt radio station in Lititz, Pennsylvania.

Publishers split their performance royalties with the writers who have contracted with them. The customary split of performance royalties (and all other royalties) between a publisher and a writer is 50/50.

Choosing which PRO to join is essentially a matter of personal taste. Each has its good features and not so great features. I choose to join ASCAP because I always admired and remembered the fancy member certificate my junior high music teacher, Charlie McNally, had hanging in the band room at Tamanend Junior High. By the time I got around to joining, ASCAP had discontinued the issuance of those fancy certificates! Oh well.

Join SoundExchange

Register yourself and your recordings with SoundExchage. SoundExchange is a non-profit that collects Digital Performance Royalties. Digital Performance Royalties are paid to featured performers and the companies or individuals who own the copyright of the sound recording. Sound Recording Copyright Owners (SRCOs) are usually record labels, like the one you just established. SoundExchage collects and distributes royalties for non-interactive digital transmissions, including satellite radio and Internet radio services, like SiriusXM, Pandora, TuneIn and Slacker Radio. Digital Performance Royalties are not directly paid to session musicians or singers. Non-featured session players are entitled to royalties that are paid through the AFM and AFTRA (American Federation of Television and Radio Artists) Intellectual Property Rights Distribution Fund.

Get onto SoundCloud and an Online Store

Place your recording on SoundCloud.

SoundCloud is an online audio distribution platform that allows subscribers to upload their recordings and to sell them worldwide. In placing your recordings on SoundCloud, be sure to enter the metadata for your tracks. The metadata for released recordings includes the publishing company name, the copyright date and the ISRC, the International Standard Recording Code, a unique number that is assigned to each recording so that it can be identified and its use tracked, worldwide.

You will also want to include a "buy" button in your SoundCloud upload. This will redirect listeners to an on-line store where folks can purchase a download of your recording. On-line retailers of digital download (and CDs) include iTunes, CDBaby and Amazon. Other websites where one can sell downloads, like ReverbNation and BandCamp, provide additional services for creative musicians including social media-type "friending" or "liking." These services help facilitate the cultivation and tracking of a fan base and are well worth exploring.

Send to Synch Publishing Specialists

Submit the master recording of your song to publishers who specialize in the business of obtaining synchronization licensing for SRCOs for placements with film and television producers. If you have established your own publishing company, the companies that specialize in synch publishing will become your sub-publisher. Contracts with synch-only sub-publishers are usually non-exclusive. That means that you can contract with several synch-only publishers and other sub-publishers who specialize in other sectors of the music publishing business, like those who handle record releases or print publishing.

Companies that specialize in synchronization-only publishing include, Crucial Music, Music Dealers, Jingle Punks. Synch-only publishing companies divide equally with the SRCO the synchronization fees that they garner. Since synch-only publishing or sub-publishing agreements are non-exclusive, this means that you could negotiate with more than one publisher to represent your copyrights. There is a big downside to having multiple companies represent you, because they all might try to pitch your same song to the same producer. Having this happen will cause ill feelings and will create lots of confusion.

There is another major drawback to working with a synch-only publisher who offers a non-exclusive contract. All synch-only publishers who work on a non-exclusive basis (where they allow you to have the same song represented by multiple publishers) do what is called, "re-titling." This means that they will rename your baby.

Let's say that the master recording and song you publish with a non-exclusive synch-only publisher is originally entitled, "Sweet Thelma Sue." Each synch-only publisher with whom you contract will add a slightly different twist to your song title. The new name one company uses might be something like "Sweet Thelma 4498" while a second company might call your song, "Thelma Sue002." The synch-only publishers rename songs in their catalog so they can be assured of receiving their share of any performance royalties that accrue from a placement they obtain. This is good, because theoretically, they will not receive payments for any recordings of your song that play on the radio or for placements they did not get.

Some find this entire process distasteful and eschew it. Other writers and SRCOs accept the synch-only business's peculiarities because they understand that by working with non-exclusive synch-only publishers they have been able to access the ears of film, television and broadcast commercial producers who would otherwise never hear their songs. If you do choose to pursue this kind of publishing or sub-publishing, it will be best to place a production with only one company at a time to avoid confusion and ill feelings.

Like many career decisions, choosing to work with or not work with a non-exclusive synch-only publisher will truly depend on where you are in your career. One must begin somewhere. The kind of exposure that one can garner from a placement in a feature film, hit television show or network commercial is career altering and is certainly much better than performing free at the local coffee shop or being punched in the chest by an irritated harpist.

SUBMIT TO A PUBLISHING SYNCHRONIZATION SPECIALIST

Submit your master recording to a music publishing synchronization specialist like Terrorbird Media, Lip Sync Music or Music Alternatives. These companies are also in the business of pitching master recordings of great songs to television producers and filmmakers, but they do not take any ownership of your copyrights. Instead, they act as publisher's agents and earn a fee for their services of between twenty and twenty-five percent of your revenues. As you can imagine, it is much more difficult to make the cut with companies like these. Because you retain all publishing rights, earn publisher's royalties and writer's royalties, a relationship with a company that acts as your agent, as do the companies mentioned here, can be much more valuable.

SELL MUSIC AT YOUR GIGS

Sell your recordings at your engagements. The do-it-yourself business model I am presenting in this scenario allows for the likelihood that, in addition to writing great songs, you are a reasonably convincing performer. If you are, and if you are successfully booking performances, you will be well served to have physical copies of your recordings available to sell when you perform. Like other aspects of the recording business, preparing physical copies of your master recording, including compact discs and vinyl LPs, has become democratized. Before the personal computer and the Internet, only large companies and a few significantly solvent individuals could afford to purchase the large minimum orders required by pressing plants.

Today, master files can be transmitted to pressing plants on the other side of the world via the Internet, cover art can quickly be designed, approved and printed on-line and finished products can be delivered in a day or two. Best of all, the manufacturing can be completed at a cost that is manageable by many.

Another method for selling your musical wares at your performances is to purchase download cards. Download cards are credit card-sized vouchers that provide an access code customers use when downloading your recordings from a special Internet site. There are many compact disc replicators, such as DiscMakers, OasisDisc, EasyDisc and NationWideDisc, who do good work. Many also offer for sale download cards and other promotional items.

STEP B: IF YOU WANT TO BE REPRESENTED BY A MAJOR PUBLISHING COMPANY

To convince a major publisher that you are worthy of their investment of time and money, you will generally be well served to have two things in addition to your talent and a great songs. It will be very helpful to be represented by a music business attorney and to have a track record of music business success.

This is all very tricky. It is difficult to have a track record if you are just starting out and it is almost impossible to have a record business lawyer put time into representing you to large publishers unless you have already made a bit of a splash in the business.

One way to establish yourself is to follow the plan for self-publishing I provided in Step A, above.

You will need to have a good quality, but not necessarily radio-ready quality recording of your potential hit song.

Next, I suggest some real reflection about what it is you have created: What kind of song did you write? What artists would sing your song?

Then, after you have determined who might do well to record your song, find out who has published that artist's last two or three songs. With a little detective work, you can find out the names of the publishers. One thing you can do is to look at the chart listings in *Billboard Magazine*. Each song listed in the magazine's charts will include names of the writers, the publisher and their performing rights organization (PRO) affiliation (ASCAP, BMI or SEASAC). You can next find the contact information for the publishing company by looking them up on the Internet or calling the PRO. PROs are generally very helpful in this regard and will readily tell you the address of their publisher members.

You will next need to write to the publishing company to ask permission to send in a demonstration recording of your song. This is because music publishers will not listen to, or even open packages from, writers who are unknown to them. This is where having a lawyer with great contacts in the music business really can help to speed up the process. An attorney who has negotiated publishing agreements with major publishers will likely be able to pick up the telephone and ask for an appointment with a publishing executive for whom you can perform your best songs live and in person.

Do not despair if you do not have a hotshot lawyer on your team. You can contact the company yourself.

First, you will need to compose a short, well-written business letter to ask permission to send your songs for their review (Example 82). Address the letter to the appropriate contact person at the publishing company office. This is probably the professional manager, but you will do well to phone the company to determine the correct name and title of the person to whom you should send your request and ultimately your songs.

Your business letter should be correct in its form, spelling and grammar. Do not write as you might speak to a band mate or buddy at the gym. Remember, you are writing to accomplished businesspersons who will be dissuaded from doing business with you if you come off like a goof at the local rock joint. They will be much more impressed and willing to listen to your demos if you conduct yourself with standard business decorum and blow their socks off with your utterly outrageous music.

If you can honestly include in your letter positive reactions to your songs, do so. "My Aunt Martha loves it," is not helpful. However, telling the professional manager that your songs are presently being played on thus-and-such radio stations will probably help pique their interest.

NOTE
Business letters are just that – business, and should strike a tone of pleasant regard for the recipient and his time.

Example 82: Business Letter

Mr. Robert Smith
Smith Music Publishing, Inc.
777 Outta Dasky Street
New York, NY 00001

December 6, 2014

Dear Mr. Smith:

I am writing you this afternoon to ask permission to send to you some of my original songs for your review for publishing.

I have experienced very good reaction to these new songs whenever they are performed. Two of my songs are presently in regular rotation and receiving airplay on WXXX, WYYY and WAAA.

For your convenience, I am including the enclosed self-addressed, postage paid post card. Please just indicate if you will review my songs and return the card to me at your earliest opportunity.

Thank you,

Samuel Songsmith

Samuel Songsmith
333 Chord change Boulevard
Bluesville Park, Pennsylvania 77777

Your next step is to mail your request for permission letter to the publishing company's professional manager. Along with your letter, you need to include a simple way for the publisher's manager to respond to your request.

One way to accomplish this is to include a self-addressed, postage paid post card (Example 83). On it, ask the professional manager to respond to the simple question, "Will you listen to my music?" and ask them to return the postcard to you.

Mention in your letter that the postcard is already addressed and that there is postage on it. The card could look something like this:

Example 83: Permission Request Postcard

Ms. Jane Smith
Big Music Publishing Company
44 Hit Song Street
Big City, USA

January 15, 2010

Dear Ms. Smith:

I would like to send you some of my songs for you to consider for publication by your company. May I?

Just check:

_____ Yes _____ No

I have already put postage on this card and addressed it to myself. I would appreciate it very much if you would mail it back to me.

Thank you,

Sonja Songwriter
Sonja Songwriter
(304) 345-6789

Ms. Sonya Songwriter
32 Lyric Way
Oh Gosh Golly Holler, WV
26222

You could also conduct this business transaction via e-mail if the receptionist tells you that the professional manager prefers to do business that way. In that case, keep it short, professional and pleasant.

Example 84: Permission Request E-mail

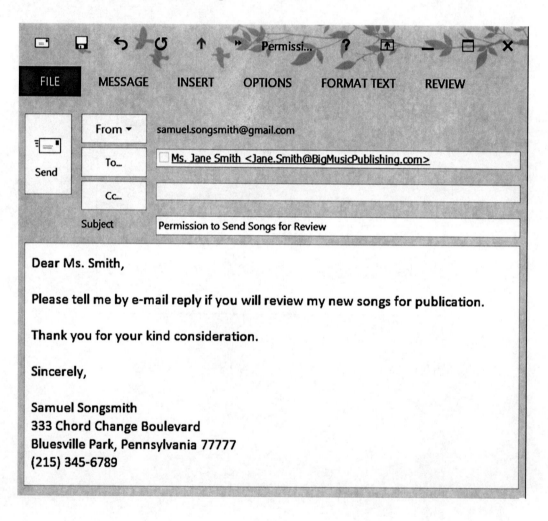

Some Final Thoughts About the Music Business

In this chapter, I have offered my ideas about why people compose songs, ways in which they can develop an income from their writing and some traditional and non-traditional paths to success. I have also included the job titles and job descriptions of the persons involved in a songwriter's successful career. There are some other very important business practitioners you will want to have on your team as you journey to songwriting profitable.

Attorneys

While it is quite true that all lawyers are created equal, it is even more true and much more important as a songwriter to recognize that not just any attorney can navigate the sometimes perilous waters of the entertainment business. As the songwriting business shares essential characteristics with other businesses (e.g., there are contracts, rights, property, negotiations, and so on), the vernacular language and common practices of entertainment business law are quite particular, if not peculiar, to that field alone. It is therefore generally wise for songwriters to work with an attorney who is well acquainted with the special requirements of working with intellectual property ownership, personal management contracts, record master lease agreements, copyrights, publishing and the general care and feeding of the creative musical artist. General practice lawyers may balk at provisions of entertainment contracts that are in fact standard practices in the music industry.

It is great to be connected with a lawyer who is regularly involved in negotiating agreements with major players in the music business. Often, that lawyer will be in a position to recommend talent to a publisher or label, or will know of a potential opportunity for a songwriter who is a client. This is perhaps the most important thing an entertainment attorney brings to the artist/attorney relationship.

Of course, the major rub is this: Young songwriters usually know little about music business contracts and law on the one hand, and on the other, usually have little or no funds to hire an attorney. The image that comes immediately to mind is the wolf eyeing up the cute little lambs in the meadow. There are many music business wolves lurking around every recording studio and publishing company just waiting to pounce on the next cute little talented writer. Short of having an established music business lawyer recognize your earnings potential and take you under his or her wing, there is little a new songwriter can do to protect himself.

There are many music business wolves lurking around every recording studio and publishing company just waiting to pounce on the next cute little talented writer.

Lori Landew, an entertainment law specialist who works in New York and Philadelphia, provided these thoughts when I asked her to comment on the dilemma of the impoverished artist who needs to consult with an experienced attorney:

> "You pose a very difficult question. I know that when artists are trying to make ends meet, scraping together money to pay for a lawyer is not going to be high on their list of priorities. It's probably a notch or two below paying for insurance for gear or instruments. However, it's hard to ignore how important good legal advice from an experienced entertainment lawyer can be, particular where an artist's rights are concerned.

> "One affordable resource that exists in many major cities is collectives of attorneys who will work with artists on a pro bono basis. In Philadelphia, for example, there is PVLA – Philadelphia Volunteer Lawyers for the Arts. PVLA works with some of the best attorneys in town who are eager to help developing artists who would not otherwise be able to afford their services.

> "Another approach is to see if you can work out an alternative billing arrangement with an attorney such as a payment plan or some kind of hybrid between an hourly fee for services and a back-end participation in the proceeds from any deal that the attorney negotiates.

> "And while I would never advocate foregoing legal advice entirely, if an artist cannot find a way to involve an attorney in his/her business, I would recommend consulting with more experienced artists. They may be able to offer some insight into how deals should work and what to watch out for so that the artist can take those insights into the contract discussions. The artist should always have the party offering the deal explain (line-by-line, if necessary) what their agreement says and why each term is there.

> "Finally, NEVER sign anything before you've read it, understand what it means and assessed the pros and cons of signing."

Landew mentions the Volunteer Lawyers for the Arts (www.vlany.org) in her comment. This non-profit organization, established in 1969, provides legal aid and educational programs about the legal and business issues that affect musical artists and others at any stage in their career. The VLA has branches throughout the country, especially in larger urban areas. A quick Internet search will likely help you find a nearby VLA office and an experienced entertainment attorney who is willing to help you at little or no cost to you.

In the best case, one should at the very least have a credible music business lawyer read any publishing or production agreement that is presented to you for your signature. One should never sign anything without having someone more knowledgeable and experienced in the entertainment business read it through.

The well-informed songwriter will also have a working knowledge of general business and know some of the specifics of the music business. Many community colleges, for instance, offer non-credit classes in business law basics for small business owners. And guess what? If you want to be in the songwriting business, you will own your own small business called, you — the songwriter!

CONSIDER JOINING THE SONGWRITERS GUILD OF AMERICA

The Songwriters Guild of America (SGA) was originally organized in 1931 as the "Songwriters Protective Association" to provide songwriters with collective strength in their dealings with the large corporate publishers, record companies, producers and studios. The SGA provides very reasonably priced membership to its large membership of published and non-published songwriters. It provides many valuable services, including workshops, social and networking events and song pitching events attended by major publishers. Among SGA's most valuable services is its ongoing lobbying for refinements to the Copyright Law and the contract review service it provides its members.

For more information, visit www.songwritersguild.com

YOU ARE A SMALL BUSINESS

To be in the songwriting business one must commit to doing all the same activities as any other owner of a small business. These include marketing, sales, negotiations, record keeping, correspondence, personnel management, banking and accounting. This is a lot of stuff to know. You will do well to consult with a certified accountant, a marketing professional and so on. There are professionals in most cities that specialize in these fields. The wise songwriting professional will model his business after those of other professional practitioners, like attorneys, builders or physicians. At its core, though, is the thorough knowledge of and a better than average talent in the craft of putting words and music together in a manner that people want to hear. Be good at music first. You can later become OK at the rest or surround yourself with persons who are.

CODA

In this text, I have provided lots of grist for your creative songwriting mill. You now have many of the basic building blocks you need to create your own songs.

You've seen how scales and chords are the important elements needed to create melodies and how chords provide the harmonic accompaniment

I have demonstrated how lyrics have to be single-minded and how they need to fit precisely the rhythm and accent pattern of the melody. Finally, I have provided you with much of the essential information you will need to work in the songwriting business.

Your assignment—have fun with what you now know. Play through the song fragments provided in this text. Sing the melodies. I know—you do not play so well and your singing leaves a lot to the imagination, right? Wrong. It doesn't matter at what level you perform right now. What matters is that you understand the general concepts I have presented and that you play through and sing a lots of great songs.

Try putting together some of the chord progressions I have introduced. See what comes up. Perhaps as you play through your new chord progression, you will think of a melody. Sometimes it happens like that.

As a teenager, I learned a lot about songwriting by playing through songs from "fake books": anthologies of songs written in lead sheet fashion. Most fake books (like the Real Book series and others) provide very good chord charts that illustrate how to form all the chords used in the songs in their collection. I've provided such a chart in the Appendix. Any time you can spend playing through songs that are well written is time well spent. In doing so, you are truly learning from masters. If you apply some of the analysis techniques I have shared with you in this text, you will learn even more.

APPENDIX

In Appendices 9.1, 9.2 and 9.3 I present the scales and chords commonly found in pop songs.

In Appendices 9.4, 9.5, and 9.6 I present several common chord progressions. Mine is by no means a complete or even thorough compendium of harmonic motion. These are truly just *some* of the many, many ways chords can progress one to another.

The chord progressions I present can serve as "song starters." I suggest you play around with them. Have fun combining them and otherwise varying them. See what you can come up with. There just might be a hit song awaiting your discovery, hiding amongst the appendices!

SCALES

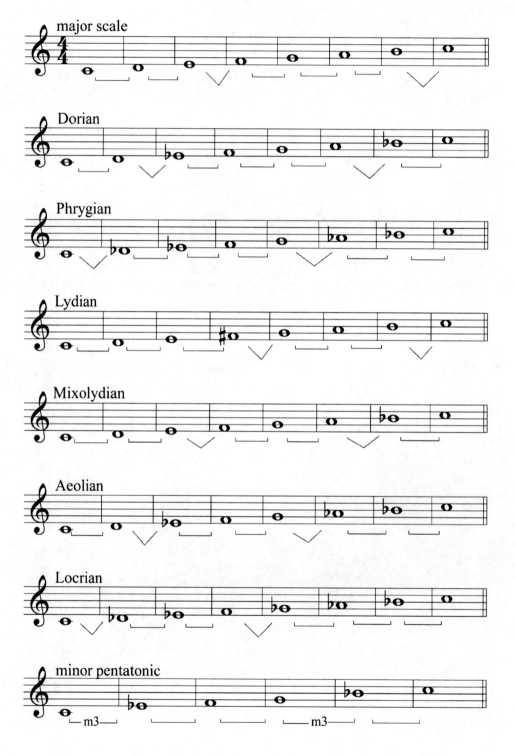

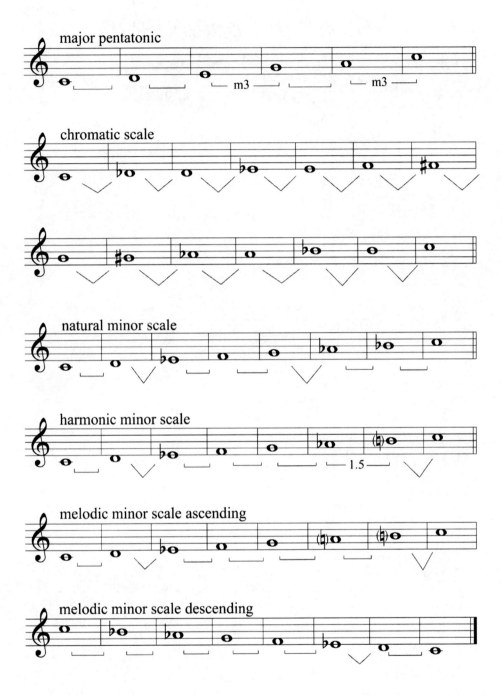

SCALES IN COMPARISON

C major scale — Relative minor: A-natural minor — Parallel minor: C-natural minor

Db major scale — Relative minor: Bb-natural min. — Parallel minor: Db-natural minor

D major scale — Relative minor: B-natural minor — Parallel minor: D-natural minor

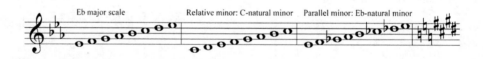

Eb major scale — Relative minor: C-natural minor — Parallel minor: Eb-natural minor

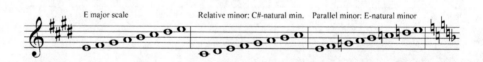

E major scale — Relative minor: C#-natural min. — Parallel minor: E-natural minor

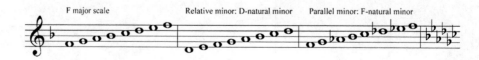

F major scale — Relative minor: D-natural minor — Parallel minor: F-natural minor

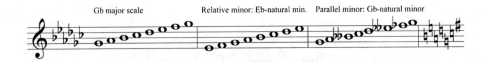

Gb major scale   Relative minor: Eb-natural min.   Parallel minor: Gb-natural minor

G major scale   Relative minor: E-natural minor   Parallel minor: G-natural minor

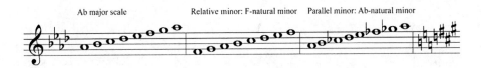

Ab major scale   Relative minor: F-natural minor   Parallel minor: Ab-natural minor

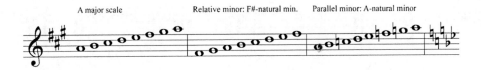

A major scale   Relative minor: F#-natural min.   Parallel minor: A-natural minor

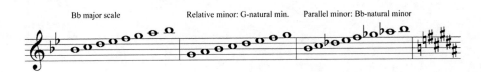

Bb major scale   Relative minor: G-natural min.   Parallel minor: Bb-natural minor

B major scale   Relative minor: G#-natural minor   Parallel minor: B-natural minor

COMMON CHORD SYMBOLS

Alternate chord symbols: *Chord symbol notation is not precisely codified. Here are some alternates you might run into.(These apply to all keys.)*

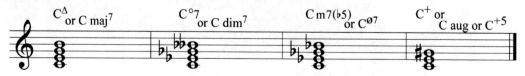

COMMON CHORD PROGRESSIONS IN MINOR

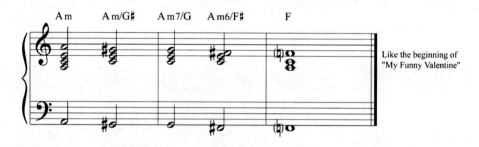

Like the beginning of
"My Funny Valentine"

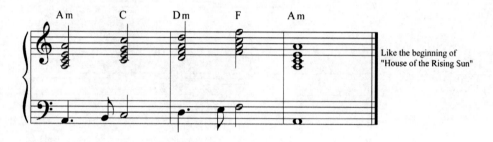

Like the beginning of
"House of the Rising Sun"

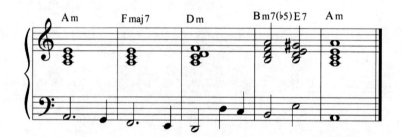

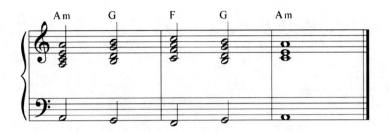

COMMON CHORD PROGRESSIONS IN MAJOR

This pattern features a tonic pedal

Brackets [ ] indicate a secondary dominant: "five of" some chord.

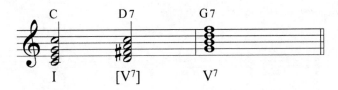

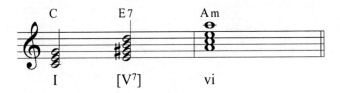

Like the end of "Silly Love Song"

Diatonic circle of fourths beginning on ii[7]

Circle of Perfect Fourths

(Enharmonic spelling: F#   Cb)

GLOSSARY

A Glossary of terms used in this book.

Term	Definition
added note chord	A triad plus an extra added pitch, most often a second, fourth, sixth, ninth, eleventh or thirteenth above the root. Pitches added above the seventh are sometimes called extensions.
Aeolian mode	One of the eight modes of the medieval Roman Catholic Church, originally spanning the octave from a to a^1 with its intervals following the pattern: whole step, half step, whole step, whole step, half step, whole step, whole step.
album	A collection of recorded music
anacrusis	One or more notes that occur before the first metrically strong beat of a musical phrase. Also called a pick-up note.
andante	A tempo indication of music instructing the performer to play a piece or section of a piece of music at a "walking speed," that is, moderately slow: from about 76 to 108 beats per minute.

Term	Definition
antecedent	The first of two complimentary phrases of music followed by a consequent phrase; also called the question with the consequent called the answer.
anthem	An inspirational song that becomes identified with and emblematic of an entity: a country, a corporation, a product, etc…Also, a religious song with a Biblical text sung as part of a church service.
augmented	Intervals: When a perfect or major interval is made larger by one half-step. Harmony: A major triad whose chord fifth is raised one half-step.
binary form	A composition made up of two interdependent periods.
block chord	Three or more pitches, usually thirds, stacked one on another and played simultaneously.
Blues Form	A single-period strophic song form of twelve or sixteen measures. Its melody is usually composed using the blues or jazz scale and is harmonized using the primary chords of the major or minor key, each with an added minor seventh.
blues scale	Also called the jazz scale, One of several six-, seven-, eight or nine-note pitch collection. It distinctively features alternate versions of scale degree three, four and seven.
borrowed	Also called modal mixture or modal interchange. The process of harmonizing a melody with a chord found in the parallel minor or major key. For instance, using the minor subdominant in a major key.

Term	Definition
bridge	An inconsequential phrase that is placed between two more significant sections of music. Bridges usually do not include musical or lyrical material that is highly developed or that adds significantly to the development of the song. Usually in stylistic contrast to the verse and chorus periods.
buyout production music library model	A recorded anthology of (usually) instrumental music produced for exclusive use in broadcast and marketing productions licensed with a one-time fee that yields no residual payments.
call-and-response	A compositional and performance technique where one artist or group of performers will present a musical fragment that will be either replicated or responded to by a second artist or group of performers.
choir music	Also choral music; music composed for an ensemble of singers.
chord	Three or more pitches arranged vertically and sounded more or less simultaneously.
chord fifth	Also simply, the fifth; The top most voice of a triad in root position; the interval of a fifth above the root.
chord of resolution	The culmination of a cadence; in a melodic cadence, the note of resolution.
chord substitution	The replacement of certain chords with others that the arranger deems to be more appropriate for the assignment at hand; re-harmonization.
chord third	Also, the third; The middle voice of a triad in root position; the interval of a third above the chord root.

Term	Definition
chorus	A period that recurs sung each time with the same lyrics. The chorus usually contains the title of the song. Also known as the refrain, hammer, sing-along and channel.
chromatic scale	A scale that divides an octave into semitones or half steps.
circular phrase	A phrase that begins and ends on a tonic harmony.
Columbia Harmony (also called the Pilgrim's Musical Companion)	The anthology written by Charles Spilman and Benjamin Shaw.
consequent	The second of two complimentary phrases; also called the answer.
consonant intervals	Intervals of major and minor thirds, perfect fifths and major and minor sixths.
development	The compositional process of variation in melody, rhythm, and harmony.
diatonic chords	Chords composed exclusively of major or minor scale tones stacked in thirds.
diegetic music	Music in a film that appears to be emanating from some element of the action on the screen; e.g., the music that appears to come from the on-screen radio or orchestra.
diminished	A minor or perfect interval when made smaller by one half step is said to be diminished.
dissonant intervals	Intervals of a second, fourth or seventh.

Term	Definition
dominant preparatory chords	The chords that resolve to the dominant, most often the chord of the supertonic or the subdominant, but also the diminished seventh chord constructed on the half step below the dominant ant the major triad (or dominant seventh chord) built on the flatted sixth.
Dorian mode	One of the eight modes of the medieval Roman Catholic Church, originally spanning the octave from d to d¹ with its intervals following the pattern: whole step, half step, whole step, whole step, whole step, half step, whole step.
dyads	A two-note chord. In pop music, a power chord composed of a triad without the third.
enharmonically equivalent	Pitches that are named differently but represent the same frequency. For example, Ab and G#.
environmental music	Background music played by in shopping malls, restaurants, and at work places.
first inversion	A chord with its third in the bass.
folk	Music that has come down to us through the years as part of an oral tradition passed from one generation to the next, whose author is unknown.
form	Within the context of our present study, the term is used to define the order, repetition and development of musical phrases.
grand rights	Performance rights granted by the composer and lyricist to the producers of musical theater and operatic works.
Great American Songbook	Also called, "standards," the name given to the loosely defined collection of songs created for Broadway and Hollywood musical of the 1930s, '40s and '50s.

Term	Definition
half cadence	A harmonic progression that resolves on the dominant.
harmonic intervals	Intervals that occur simultaneously (vertically).
Harmonice musices odhecaton	The first collection of music printed entirely from movable type. Published by Ottaviano Petrucci (1466-1539) of Venice in 1501.
historical bar form	A form of musical composition that follows the formal musical design, AAB.
hook	In pop music (especially recordings), any short lyrical, melodic or rhythmic fragment that provides a composition or recording a distinctively unique and memorable sonic point of reference.
intellectual property	The product of an artistic endeavor. In the music business, songs and recordings are construed as intellectual property. Like other kinds of property, intellectual property can be owned, sold, rented, stolen or given away.
intertextual	For our purposes, the interrelationship between one piece of music and another, understanding that all music references some other preexisting piece of music.
interval	The distance between two pitches when counting on the musical alphabet.
introductory verse	A rambling sixteen to thirty-two measure period whose lyric provides a context for the song that is to follow. The introductory verse sets the stage for the singer to unfold the story of the song proper.
Ionian mode	A scale whose organization of tones and semitones follows the same pattern as the major scale, e.g., the collection of pitches from C^3 to C^4.

Term	Definition
jingle production houses	Companies market the works of their employees who are charged with composing and producing recorded music for advertising and marketing.
key of the moment	A temporary tonic
lining out	A tradition of choral recitation, where the leader reads a line and the congregation repeats it in unison, or where the leader sings a line that is then repeated. Also called call-and-response.
Locrian mode	A scalar collection whose interval relationship mimics the diatonic collection from b to b^1, with pitches organized as follows: half step, whole step, whole step, half step, whole step, whole step, whole step.
Lydian mode	One of the eight modes of the medieval Roman Catholic Church, originally spanning the octave from a to a1 with its intervals following the pattern: whole step, whole step, whole step, half step, whole step, whole step, half step.
lyrical hook	A short memorable word phrase.
major pentatonic scale	A five-note scale whose intervals follow the pattern: whole step, whole step, minor third, whole step, minor third.
major third	An interval of 4 half steps.
measure	Also called a bar. A unit of time in music determined by the prevailing meter signature and represented in manuscript as the space between two bar lines.
mechanical licenses	A legal agreement issued by a publisher that grants a record company permission to record a composition published by the publisher.
mechanical royalty	The fee paid by a record company to a publisher for the license of their intellectual property.

Term	Definition
melisma	A single syllable accompanied by a group of more than a one note.
melodic intervals	Intervals that occur in succession
melodic motive/hook	A short, rhythmically impressive and memorable melodic fragment.
meter	Music occurs in time that is measured by beats, an even succession of metrical pulses, like the sound that is made when one marches. The pulses are organized in groups, most commonly in groups of two, three or four. Other groupings, including five, six, seven, nine, and twelve, are also found in Western music.
meter signature	Also called the time signature. The fractional number that is placed at the beginning of the composition or section thereof. The denominator of the time signature indicates the basic note value of the meter (what note value receives the basic beat of the piece). The numerator indicates the number of note values in a measure (the number of beats found in each measure).
minor pentatonic scale	A five-note scale whose intervals follow the pattern: minor third, whole step, whole step, minor third, whole step.
minor third	An interval of three half steps.
Mixolydian mode	One of the eight modes of the medieval Roman Catholic Church, originally spanning the octave from g to g¹ with its intervals following the pattern: whole step, whole step, half step, whole step, whole step, half step, whole step.
modal	Music based on the Gregorian modes (as opposed to major, minor, or other scales), including the Dorian, Phrygian, Lydian, mixolydian, and Aeolian.

Term	Definition
moderato	A moderate tempo between andante (a walking tempo) and allegro (fast).
musical contour	The shape of a melody, specifically, how it moves higher and lower
musical period	A complete musical statement in tonal music that ends in a harmonic cadence that requires no immediate further resolution.
musical phrase	A unit of music that is self-contained. It is heard as a complete musical statement with a beginning, middle and end, concluding with a final harmonic and melodic cadence that requires no further resolution. A phrase in music is analogous to a clause in language.
musicals	A play or movie where the action is moved forward through singing and dancing. Made popular in the 20th century in England and the U.S. musical theater is related to operetta, comic opera and the revue.
numerical size	Intervals are measured in terms of their numerical size, that is, the number of letter names the two tones span when counting on the musical alphabet.
octave (perfect octave)	An interval of 11 half steps, for instance from middle C to the C eight scale steps higher.
Olney Hymns	A collection in which the Reverend John Newton's poem, "Amazing Grace," was first published in 1779.
opening phrase	A musical phrase whose final cadence resolves on the dominant.
pentatonic scale	Any of several five note scales, most commonly following the same ordering as the black keys of the piano beginning on either the e-flat (for the minor pentatonic), or the g-flat (for the major pentatonic).

Term	Definition
perfect authentic cadence	The harmonic progression of dominant to tonic where the melody moves from scale step seven to scale step eight.
perfect consonances	Intervals of perfect octaves and perfect fifths.
performance royalties	Fees collected by a PRO and paid to the copyright owner for the public performance of a composition. Fees are shared equally by the writers and the publisher.
Performing Rights Organizations (PROs)	Organizations that to collect and distribute performance fees to publishers and writers. In the U.S. these include ASCAP, BMI and SESAC.
Phrygian mode	One of the five original modes of the Roman Church, its pitches proceed step-wise as: half, whole, whole, whole, half, whole, whole.
pillar/primary chords	The tonic, subdominant, and dominant harmonies of the tonal system. The I, IV and V chords.
pop music	Any of many genres that are successful in the commercial marketplace, including country, folk, jazz, adult contemporary, r & b, and rock.
Pop Song Binary Form	One of three binary form configurations. Usually thirty two measures long, divided into two distinct sixteen-measure periods. Each sixteen-measure period consists of two balanced eight measure phrases, labeled A, B and C. Each eight-measure phrase, A, B and C, is commonly divided into two four-measure sub-phrases, where the A-phrase repeats at the beginning of the second period.

Term	Definition
production music library	A collection of music produced and licensed by its publisher for exclusive use background music in broadcast commercials, television programs, educational, motivational, and corporate films. The compositions in a production music library are not licensed for use in entertainment, like commercially released recordings.
prosody	The rhythm of language.
push marketing	A form of marketing where an advertiser creates demand for a product or service through repeated media advertising. This contrasts with "pull marketing," where demand for a product or service is the result of buyers perceived needs.
quality	The sonic characteristic assigned to define further an interval's nature, including major, minor, perfect, augmented and diminished.
quartal harmony	Harmony based on combinations of fourths rather than thirds (tertian harmony).
radio station i.d.s / shotgun announcements / sweepers	Very short musical logos designed to provide a quickly recognizable sonic identification for a radio or television station or network.
remote key	A key other than the relative key, the key of the dominant or the subdominant.
rhyme scheme	The pattern of the rhyming words of a poem or song lyric. When lyricists place rhymes at the end of a line of text, this is called an *end rhyme* or *terminal rhyme*. When a lyricist rhymes a word in the middle of a line of text with the last word of a line or if two words in the middle of a line rhyme, it is called an *internal rhyme* or a *middle rhyme*.

Term	Definition
riff / lick	Melodic, rhythmic or harmonic motives that occur in the accompaniment; hooks.
root position	A chord voiced with its root in the bass.
rounded binary form	A form of compositional organization consisting of two periods, thus the binary designation, where the first period recurs after the playing of the second period. This yields a formal structure, ABA.
sawaal-javaab	Literally "call and response" in classical music of North India.
scale	The organization of a pitch collection from lowest to highest.
second inversion	A chord voiced with its fifth in the bass.
spirituals	A form of religious folk song first sung by African-Americans in the southern United States. Also called revival and camp meeting songs. Spirituals date back to the early part of the 19th century.
stop chorus	A performance style in which the rhythm section plays only the first beat of each measure while a musician plays an improvised solo.
strophic form	A single-period form characterized by lyrics that change from verse to verse over an unvaried melody.
sub-phrase	A short phrase, usually four measures long, within a phrase.
supertonic triad	A triad built on scale degree two, the supertonic.
synchronization royalties	Fees paid by the producer to the copyright owner when a piece of music is licensed for use as part of a motion picture soundtrack.
tessitura	The pitch range of a composition or a section of a composition.

Term	Definition
The Great White Way	The colloquial name for New York City's Broadway theater district.
third inversion	A chord voiced with its seventh in the bass.
time signature	The fractional number placed at the beginning of the composition or section thereof. The denominator of the time signature indicates the basic note value of the meter (what note value receives the basic beat of the piece). The numerator indicates the number of note values in a measure (the number of beats found in each measure).
tonic triad	A chord built on the first degree of the scale, where scale degree one (the tonic) is the root of the chord.
transpose	Shifting from one key center to another while retaining all the melodic and harmonic intervallic relationships.
triad	A three note chord, in the tonal system, composed of thirds.
tritone	The interval of an augmented fourth or diminished fifth; the span of three whole steps. These intervals are heard as dissonant in all cultures.
tritone substitution	In re-harmonization, using a substitute chord whose root is a tritone away from the true dominant chord for which it is the substitute. The two chords, the original and its tritone substitute, always contain the same tritone in its composition, though the notes of the interval are spelled enharmonically.
Troubadour / Trouvérs	Nobelmen singers and songwriters from southern France and northeast Spain who lived from about 1100 to 1300. The Troubadours and Trouvérs composed the first vernacular lyric songs of Europe.

Term	Definition
twelve-tone system	As distinct from the tonal system, the twelve-tone or dodecaphonic system provides a serial ordering of all twelve chromatic pitches, uniquely formed for each composition.
Twentieth Century Bar Form	The most common musical form of the first half of the twentieth century, Twentieth Century Bar Form closely resembles the formal design of the rounded binary form: AABA.
unison	The interval formed by two playing's of the same pitch; also, the simultaneous performance of a musical line, sometimes at the octave.
verse	A period that compliments and leads to the chorus. Verses are usually in strophic form, where the lyrics change from verse to verse, but the melody remains the same.
Virginia Harmony	The collection in which "New Britain," (the musical setting for John Newton's text, "Amazing Grace"), first appeared.
work-for-hire	A legal agreement wherein a creative agrees to perform or compose as part of his employment without further compensation.

REFERENCES

MUSIC EXAMPLES (CITED IN ORDER OF APPEARANCE)

YESTERDAY, John Lennon and Paul McCartney, © 1965 SONY/ATV Tunes, LLC dba ATV OBO ATV (Northern Songs Catalog).

THE GIRL FROM IPANEMA, V. de Moraes, N. Gimbel, and A.C. JOBIM, © 1962 Words West, LLC/Songs of Universal, Inc.

YOUR CHEATIN' HEART, Hank Williams, © 1953 Sony/ATV Acuff Rose Music.

PIANO MAN, Billy Joel, © 1973 Almo Music Corp./OBO Joelsongs.

WAKE ME UP WHEN SEPTEMBER ENDS, Billie Joe Armstrong & Greenday, © 2003 WB Music Corp. /OBO Green Daze Music.

BRISTOL STOMP, David Appell and Kal Mann, © 1961 Spirit Two Music/OBO Kal Mamm Music.

BLUE MOON Lorenz Hart and Richard Rogers, © 1935 EMI Robins Catalog, Inc.

CAROLINA IN MY MIND, James Taylor, © 1968 EMI Blackwood Music, Inc., EMI April Busic, Inc. OBO Country Road Music.

WHAT A WONDERFUL WORLD, G. D. Weiss, George Douglas and B. Thiele, © 1967 Range Road Music, Inc., Quartet Music, Inc., Imagen Sounds OBO Abilene Music, LLC.

JEREMY, Jeff Ament, Eddie Vedder, © 1991 Universal-Polygram International Publishing, Inc. Scribing C-ment Songs, Innocent Bystander.

JEANNIE WITH THE LIGHT BROWN HAIR, Stephen C. Foster, public domain

MY FUNNY VALENTINE, Lorenz Hart, Richard Rodgers, © 1937 Chappell & Co.

GENTLE HEART, Louis Anthony deLise, © 2014 Print Music Source

HERE'S THAT RAINY DAY, Jimmy Van Heusen, Johnny Burke, © 1949, 1953 Burke & Van Heusen, Inc, assigned to Bourne Co. and Dorsey Bros.

MY ROMANCE, Richard Rodgers, Lorenz Hart, © 1935 T.B.Harms Co.

WE DIDN'T START THE FIRE, Billy Joel, © 1989 Joelsongs

NICK & ME, Louis Anthony deLise & Phillip C. Hartman, © 2014 Bocage Music Publishing

A FINE ROMANCE, Jerome Kern & Dorothy Fields, © 1936 Universal Music Publishing Group

HELP, John Lennon & Paul McCartney, © 1965 Northern Songs, Limited

I CAN'T GIVE YOU ANYTHING BUT LOVE, Jimmy McHugh & Dorothy Fields, © 1928 Shapiro Bernstein & Co. Inc. O/B/o Aldi Music

EVERYTHING HAPPENS TO ME, Tom Adair & Matt Dennis, © 1941 Dorsey Brothers Music

PERIODICALS

Rorem, N. (1974), Why I Write As I Do. *American Music Center's Symposium on Contemporary Music, City University of New York. Tempo Magazine.*

Custodero, L.A. (2006), Singing Practices in 10 Families with Young Children. *JRME*, Vol. 54. No. 1 pp. 37-56.

Hohmann, A., Rüber, T., Schlaug , G., Wan, C.Y. (2010), The Therapeutic Effects of Singing in Neurological Disorders. *Music Perception*, 27, 4, . 287-295.

Inman, D. (2011), Industry Spotlight: The Harry Fox Agency. *The American Songwriter.*

Tolbert, E. (2001). Music and meaning: An evolutionary story. *Psychology of Music, 29* (1), 84-94.

Texts

Abbs, Peter and Richardson, John (1990). The Forms of Poetry: A Practical Study Guide. Cambridge University Press.

Aldwell, E., & Schachter, C. (1989). *Harmony and Voice Leading* (2nd ed.). New York: Harcourt Brace Jovanovich College Publishers.

Baskerville, D., & Baskerville, T. (2010). *Music Business Handbook and Career Guide* (9th ed.). Thousand Oaks, CA : Sage Publications, Inc.

Caldwallader, A., & Gagné., D. (1998). *Analysis of Tonal Music: A Schenkerian Approach.* New York: Oxford University Press.

Davis, S. (1985). *The Craft of Lyric Writing.* Cincinnati, OH: Writer's Digest Books.

Feld, S., & Neuman, D. M. (1984). *Sound and Sentiment: Birds, Weeping, Poetics, and Song in Kaluli Expression.* Durham, NC: Duke University Press.

Frank, Robert J., (2010) *Theory on the Web*, http://smu.edu/totw/melody.htm

Grout, D.J., Palisca, C. (2001). *A History of Western Music* (6th ed.). New York: W.W.Norton & Company, Inc.

The Harvard Dictionary of Music Fourth Edition ISBN 0-674-01163-5 © 1986, 2003 The Belknap Press of Harvard Univ Press

Hugh, F. (1975). *The World of Entertainment: Hollywood's Greatest Musicals.* New York: Avon Books.

Jackson, G.P. (Ed.) (1964). *Spiritual Folk-Songs of Early America*

Jaffe, Andrew. (1983). *Jazz Theory.* Dubuque, IA: Wm. C. Brown Company Publishers.

Klein, M.L. (2005). *Intertextuality in Western Art Music.* Bloomington, IN: Indiana University Press.

Laitz, S.G. (2008). *The Complete Musician* (2nd ed.). New York: Oxford University Press.

Levitin, D. J. (2006). *This is Your Brain on Music.* New York, NY: Plume Books.

Lomax, A., Asch, M. (Eds.) (1962). *The Leadbelly Songbook.* New York: Oak Publications.

Orem, P. W. (1924). *Theory and Composition of Music*, Theodore Presser Co. Phila.

Pattison, P. (1991). *Songwriting: Essential Guide to Lyric Form and Structure.* Boston: Berklee Press.

Pere, B. (2010). *Songcrafters' Coloring Book.* Mystic, CT: Creative Songwriting Academy Press.

Pinsky, R. and Dietz, M. (2006). An Invitation to Poetry. W.W.Norton & Co.

Tolbert, E. (2001). Music and meaning: An evolutionary story. Psychology of Music, 29(1), 84-94.

Turek, R. (2007). *Theory for Today's Musician.* New York: McGraw-Hill.

Webb, J. (1998). *Tunesmith: Inside the Art of Songwriting.* New York: Hyperion.

Finale® Owners Manual (2014). Eden Prairie, MN: Make Music

INTERVIEWS

Lori Landew, Partner and Co-Chair, Fox Rothschild, LLP. Philadelphia, PA.

Joseph Renzetti, Academy Award-winning composer and arranger of many top-ten hit records. New York, NY.

WEBSITES

- Harry Fox Agency - http://www.harryfox.com
- Mood Media - http://www.moodmedia.com
- ASCAP - http://www.ascap.com/about
- BMI - http://www.bmi.com/about
- SESAC - http://www.sesac.com/About/About.aspx
- NARAS - http://www.grammy.org
- http://www.nab.org/documents/resources/broadcastFAQ.asp
- http://en.wikipedia.org/wiki/Alphabet_song
- Tin Pan Alley - http://en.wikipedia.org/wiki/Tin_Pan_Alley
- Great American Songbook - http://en.wikipedia.org/wiki/Great_American_Songbook
- Songwriters Guild of America- http://www.songwritersguild.com

Index

CPSIA information can be obtained
at www.ICGtesting.com
Printed in the USA
FFOW01n1942081014
7904FF

9 780692 304594